A DAY IN THE LIFE OF SWEDEN

A Day in the Life of Sweden is the largest photographic project in Swedish history.
It was made possible with the generous support of the following companies:

MAIN SPONSORS
HP Posten SEB

PARTNERS
**Atlas Copco Big Image Bird & Bird Dagens Nyheter Diabolaget
First Hotels FOTO Fujifilm Pressens Bild Securitas Svenskt Papper**

© Bokförlaget Max Ström
© Photographs: the individual photographers
Executive director: Jeppe Wikström
Managing editor: Lars Fahlén
Text: Petter Karlsson
Translation: Kim Loughran
Design: Patric Leo
Printed on Silverblade matt 150 gsm
Colour separation and printing: Fälth & Hässler, Värnamo, Sweden 2003
Binding: Fälth & Hässler, Farsta, Sweden
ISBN: 91-89204-65-4

3 000 PHOTOGRAPHERS — 24 HOURS

A DAY IN THE LIFE OF SWEDEN

BOKFÖRLAGET MAX STRÖM

CONTENTS

This day, a life

It was the day that three-year-old Raoul Ek disappeared in the park.

Grandma turned her head for a few seconds and when she looked back, the boy was gone. After a minute, concern turned to worry. Then to anxiety, alarm and desperation. The unthinkable had happened. Had he been taken by a paedophile? A kidnapper? Wild thoughts swirled through grandma's head. Panic-stricken, she called the boy's parents and the three of them spread out, calling and searching. But in vain. They called the police who immediately recognized the seriousness of the situation and put several units into the hunt. It took an hour before Raoul was found hidden under the leafy branches of one of the park's huge trees. He had been taught that if lost in the forest, don't wander aimlessly about, find a tree and hug it like a giant teddy bear. Yes, he said, he had tried to shout, but his voice was little and squeaky.

An ordinary day in June.

A day like any other.

And yet not.

On the nine o'clock TV news, the top item was the oil spill in the southern Baltic following a collision between two ships; the doubling of skin cancer cases among Swedish teenagers; the three-percent drop in the value of the krona; and the weather — exceptionally beautiful: some provinces recorded 27 degrees Celsius.

But beyond the headlines was another reality.

Sometimes history is in the small, modest incidents such as a runaway three-year-old, a hole-in-one on a park minigolf course, a clarinetist playing in his basement to avoid disturbing the neighbours, or maybe a dog creeping under the covers to snuggle up to its sleeping mistress.

The third of June, 2003 …

In the beginning was the Word perhaps, but the memory of this Tuesday will be in the Pictures.

In a hundred years, researchers will be studying these pages, going over these pictures with a magnifying glass and musing that those Swedes were a remarkable people. So colourful, so diverse, so restless, so prosperous. So fond of the sun, of dogs, water, bingo, and … cows?

Swedes may well have the reputation of being security junkies, shy, unobtrusive, and a little granola-flavoured, but in the pictures from 3 June 2003, an unmistakable joie de vivre jumps out at you.

Life loves life, the wise man said. It's as though life's energy is unstoppable: it bubbles like a geyser when kids play around a red mattress at the Lightning Bug day care outside Stockholm; it shines like a sun on the steel frames of five shopping trolleys sprinting across a parking lot outside the bargain outlets of Ullared in southern Sweden.

So this is no ordinary picture book.

A picture is worth more than a thousand research papers, pamphlets or political reports — so what can the value be of 24,000 pictures distilled down to 235.

Together they form a map, a cipher, a riddle, where the answer is the lives of a people.

At 12.07 am in this fair summertime, little Tilde first opened her beautiful eyes in the maternity ward of the Malmö General Hospital, and only about an hour later, a helicopter took 94-year-old Vera from her home in the Stockholm archipelago to hospital in Stockholm where she would later die. And as a senior citizen in Mora puts on earphones to listen to the morning news, a Swedish soldier is lighting a cigarette on an exercise area in Strängnäs. At the moment when an airforce JAS 39 Gripen sweeps past a castle in southern Sweden, a rural postal worker is delivering some of the 15,177,000 packages and letters mailed or recieved this day.

It's both magnificent and strange.

"This day, a life," wrote the Swedish 18th-century poet Thomas Thorild. And here we are, with at least a modicum of proof.

There are, believes celebrity astrophysicist Stephen Hawking, 100 million galaxies each with 100,000 million solar and planetary systems in a universe that is 20 billion years old composed of 10-to-the-power-of-77 atoms. In that perspective, we are a dismal fly-speck, a blink in the eye of eternity.

And yet …

Only here, on 3 June 2003, did a man put his two bassets on a leash to stroll along the beautiful Magle wetlands outside Hässleholm, southern Sweden. It was an historic event. No other man had previously covered that exact route, gazed at those particular flowers or thought his specific thoughts.

This day, a life; to be sure. But also a death, a party, a farewell, a tough shift on an overhead crane, a pirouette onstage at the Royal Opera that almost defies gravity, a child shedding tears after tumbling from a bike, and a mother nearly fainting when the doctor stitches a gash in her son's lip. In each instant, an eternity.

In the almost incredible time frame of one hundred and twenty-fifth of a second, perhaps even briefer, existence freezes, is sucked into a lens, morphs into pixels and is preserved for a portion of posterity.

The Voyager space probe sent off by Nasa in 1977 towards distant galaxies carries an engraved plate showing a man and a woman and a simplified map of our solar system. This book is a kind of probe and map. A call from our time that will echo into the future. Look what we did! See who we were! See us!

The third of June 2003 was perhaps a day like any other, but on another day in another time, new generations will study this 256-page guidebook to life and marvel at its span.

Sweden on 3 June 2003 sees several culture clashes that almost buckle the pages, but there is also togetherness, gentleness and a little fussing with private things. There are tragedies, death, pain, alienation and desperation — but also love, devotion, intimacy and joy that at times transcend comprehension.

Sweden — Mother Svea, as the Swedes say — is ancient and free, in the words of the national anthem and as the pictures convey, but she is reborn every midnight: a curious, wide-eyed infant ready to grapple with what we recognise as reality.

It's hard not to be humble when you see this ant-hill of people and possibilities. That so much can be squeezed inside a nation's borders; inside 449,964 in honesty, thinly populated square kilometres! That life can be so big and wide!

The third of June 2003 was the day 334 new Swedes were born.

It was also the day 234 died, 22 married, 68 divorced, 5,290 were behind bars and 92 emigrated to parts unknown, while 187 moved in the other direction, signing on as new citizens of a little Nordic kingdom which, just before midnight, had a population of exactly 8,953,111.

And it was, not least, the day when more than 3,000 photographers together took more pictures than any other day in Sweden's history.

Petter Karlsson

NIGHT

Borlänge, 1.16 am. Late-night snack. Photo: Johan Lundahl.
Stockholm, 2.30 am. Insomnia. Photo: Stefan Borgius.
Stockholm, 1.30 am. Closing time. Photo: Pontus Lundahl.
Riksgränsen, 1.25 am. Ski turn, Norwegian-style. Photo: Lars Thulin.
Tullstationen, Svinesund, 1.48 am. Truck stop. Photo: Marco Iaconelli.
Visby, 2.10 am. Night prowler. Photo: Tommy Söderlund.
Västerås, 0.50 am. Postal sorting. Photo: Lennart Hyse.
Kvarnen Restaurant, Stockholm, 1.35 am. Pub talk. Photo: Uwe Behrens.
Stenö Beach, Söderhamn, 2.33 am. Beach party. Photo: Daniel Nilsson.
Sligen, Ludvika, 4.15 am. Morning mist. Photo: Janos Jurka.

Mount Kebnekaise, 1.30 am. It's a cold summer night. The rest of the country is preparing to embrace the summer, but outside the old hut at the peak of Mount Kebnekaise white snow lies thick. During the night, a cold front has moved in from the west, forcing 21-year-old Catrin Grundsten and her father to stay zipped up in their sleeping bags the whole day. The Scandinavian mountain range is one of the oldest in the world, with its extension in the North American Appalachians. Over millions of years, the range has been ground down thousands of metres to its present, softly undulating form. The highest peak is 2,113m above sea level, first climbed by Frenchman Charles Rabot in 1883. The hut is at 1,880m. It's the highest bed in Sweden. Photo: Claes Grundsten. *Previous page.*

Maternity ward, Falun, 0.30 am. His surname is Sjöns, but his given name has yet to be given. He is under a blue daylight lamp to alleviate his infantile jaundice — a common, not especially dangerous condition for newborn babies The little cap has been pulled down to protect his eyes. All this is not entirely appreciated. Photo: Henrik Hansson.

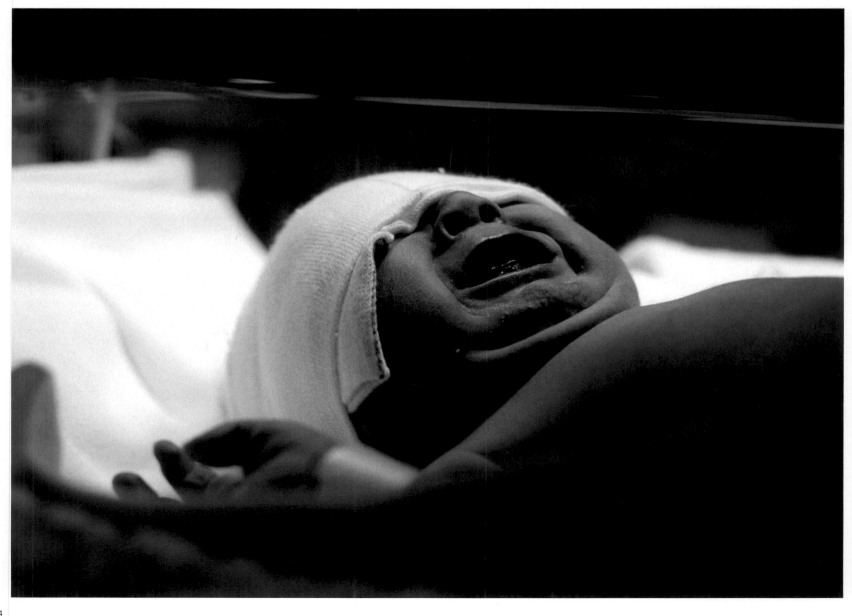

E-14 Highway, Stöde, 0.06 am. Candles burn for lives snuffed out. It's exactly five days since a dreadful accident, a few tens of kilometres west of Sundsvall. Five youths between the ages of 14 and 26 will never come home again. Flowers, letters and toy animals have been la d alongside the road in a last distraught gesture from parents, siblings and mates. Photo: Svante Berggren.

Rosengård district, Malmö, 4.02 am. Let's hope God is an early riser. Sixty-year-old Diabaté Dialy Mory gets up every morning at four to roll out his prayer mat for the first of his daily prayers to his Lord and Creator. "Dallas" Dalmory came to Sweden in the Sixties as a dancer with a Senegalese troupe. He stayed, married a Swedish girl and is today one of Fosengård district's best-known faces. Malmö has people from 165 countries; 51 percent of primary school children have immigrant origins. "I have a thousand children," says Dallas, who works as a recreation counsellor and boxing instructor for problem kids. He'l straighten out most of them, he says. With Allah's help. Photo: Torbjörn Andersson. *Next page.*

Ulvsunda industrial area and Hägerstens-åsen, 1.53–4.16 am. Her only weapons are a nightstick and an eight-year-old with a wet nose. But security guard Monica Holmgren, 36, feels safe enough since her companion is an Alasatian called Nemårs-Kamp of imposing appearance and determination. They respond to calls together — often a suspected break-in, a broken window or perhaps a suspicious shadow seen flitting through a factory area that should be locked and bolted. "It's good to have Kamp along. If there's trouble, people tend to calm down quickly when they see him." In an unsettled world, security is one of the fastest growing businesses. But there was a security industry as early as in the 17th century. "Four o'clock.

May God protect town and land from fire and pestilence," could be heard shouted out by council-employed guards patrolling the streets of Stockholm. Their main duty was to discover fire and sound the alarm. On the 17th-century guard's belt hung a brass horn — but also a large grapple to drag off drunks and other riff-raff to the lock-up. Photo: Jörgen Hildebrandt.

Shell service station, central Göteborg, 2.48 am. Sofie Hällgren works nights at an isolated downtown service station. Per Harström is a taxi driver and often swings by when he is without a fare and bored. But theirs is a love with obstacles: the shop door is locked at night for security reasons. If they want to steal a kiss, it has to be through the night hatch. On the other hand, this is where they met. She was on duty one night when he came by for petrol. It was love at first full tank. Photo: Niklas Maupoix.

Kvistberga farm, Västerås, 3.15 am. Late hours, hard work. Hans Nääf fears neither devil, troll nor wayward elk. In the light summer night he needs only one extra spotlight, but in winter, his car is lit up like a Christmas tree w th all the extra spots on the roof. Hans begins and finishes his work-day as a newspaper deliverer before soundly sleeping Swedes wake up. Photo: Lennart Hyse.

Police HQ, Kungsholmen, Stockholm, 0.04 am. At police operative headquarters, the day kicks off with a mass brawl involving football supporters following a local derby the previous evening. Big brother is keeping watch through the summer night, though. Thirteen pairs of eyes and ears are keeping track and send units to trouble spots. Soon, the bars will start closing, which will mean new disturbances. Across the country, 2,570 crimes will be reported to the police this Tuesday. Of those, 449 relate to stolen bicycles, 505 to car break-ins and 164 to picked pockets. Photo: Dag Öhrlund. *Previous page.*

Frejgatan street, Stockholm, 0.35 am. The football derby between AIK and Djurgården ended in a 3-3 draw. Afterwards, rival mobs roamed the streets of the city looking for each other. On a pedestrian crossing, the long arm of the long pins down one of the troublemakers, which acts as a signal for the mob to attack. In the tumult, a policeman's nose is broken by a boot and a female officer feels threatened enough to fire a warning shot into the air. Afterwards, her body is shaking from the shock and she is being comforted by a plain-clothes colleague. Photo: P O Sännås.

Skagerrack, off Öckerö, Skåne province, 3.45 am–3.15 pm. The trawl is playing up and suddenly, tiredness is just a memory. Although the sun's first rays have yet to drag themselves over the horizon of the inner islands, the working day has begun for west coast fishermen Kjell Olofsson and Janne Karlsson. Theirs is an ancient, tough, wet and sturdy trade. What good are super-modern devices such as sonic depth finders, radar, GPS and autopilots when equipment gets in a twist or fish have to be gutted? After dinner, it's Janne's turn to do the dishes while Kjell takes five on the bench. On the menu today was fresh haddock. Photo: Adam Ihse.

Krokvik, 1.48 am. Ingvar Mettävainio and his workmates are up at dawn to straighten out the rails along what is known as the Iron Ore Line. It's six degrees Celsius above zero, there are no mosquitoes around and it's exactly 1,420km and 250m to Stockholm's Central Station. Photo: Peter Hoelstad. *Next spread.*

EARLY MORNING

Lärkeröd, 7.23 am. Time for school. Photo: Niklas Gustavsson.
Övedskloster, Sjöbo, 5.50 am. Boar crossing. Photo: Per Sundgren.
Helsingborg, 6.30 am. Not a morning person. Photo: Ralph Nykvist.
Arlanda-Sturup, 6.45 am. Aerial breakfast. Photo: Pia Lindberg.
Göteborg, 7.50 am. Kitchen hug. Photo: Per Hanstorp.
Hågeryd, 8.22 am. Potato hilling. Photo: Lars-Olof Hallberg.
Skeppsbron, Stockholm, 9.25 am. Mobile toys. Photo: Magnus Fröderberg.
Gröningen, Helsingborg, 6.09 am. Morning dip. Photo: Roland Stregfeldt.
Royal Palace, Stockholm, 8 am. Blowing in the wind. Photo: Jessica Gow.
Huddinge, Stockholm, 8.05 am. Chimney sweep. Foto: Jan Düsing.
Halmstad, 9.56 am. Me and my dad. Photo: Anders Andersson.

Färnäs, Mora, 9.03 am. For almost 60 years, Svea and Lasås Holger Hansson have begun the day with breakfast and then a nap together. Svea makes the tea, cuts up the fruit and fixes the open sandwiches while Holger waits in bed. He likes to listen to the radio news at nine. He uses earphones so Svea won't be disturbed. Photo: Pasi Autio. *Previous page.*

TV4, Tegeluddsvägen road, Stockholm, 6.27 am. Wake up, you're on the air! It looks like TV4 breakfast show presenter Henrik Johnsson has fallen asleep during the show, but he is actually doing neck rolls to limber up. His co-anchor Elisabet Frerot is doing her own stretching while waiting for their next live spot. Breakfast TV was unknown when television broadcasts began in Sweden in 1956. Decades would come and go before Swedes had TV hosts who rose earlier than most people. Photo: Urban Andersson.

Karl Krooksgatan street, Helsingborg, 7.55 am. A lost fakir? A tourist who has been run over? A tuckered-out night owl, fallen asleep on his way home from a club? None of the above: it's Los Angeleno Kevin Owens, night porter, doing his morning exercises outside his home. "It was too hot inside. I usually try and do my exercises before eight in the morning." Photo: Torbjörn Andersson.

Blasieholm Quay, Stockholm, 4.15 am. Buenas tardes, México! President Vicente Fox is on a state visit and Mexican TV reporters have been dragged out of bed at dawn to prepare their spots for the evening news back home. It's a pool, so time is tight, and there's no room for improvisation. Each reporter gets exactly three minutes on camera. It's an almost comical procession, with five reporters in a row saying almost exactly the same thing. And all the while, the principal figure is asleep in his hotel room, waiting for the day's meetings with politicians and the Swedish royal couple. Photo: Richard Ryan. *Next page.*

Södergatan street, Malmö, 5.27 am. In a street of exclusive boutiques, a homeless man has found some junk food leftovers in a trash basket, while Heléne Moberg cleans up after last night's partying. "My dad used to be a street cleaner and I just continued the tradition." Twenty years ago, tramps, beggars and poor people were a rare sight on Swedish streets. When the business climate faltered at the end of the '90s, they came back. Sweden is again a nation with a wide rich-poor divide. Photo: Torbjörn Andersson. *Previous spread.*

Gekå Hypermarket parking lot, Ullared, 9.08 am. Wags call it "the kiddy rally", but all ages and genders do it. Shopping in the cut-rate hypermarkets in Ullared, in southern Halland province, is a pastime enjoyed by a wide cross-section — zipping through bargain bins, extra discount deals and frazzled family nerves. The pants you bought don't always fit so well when you get home. Photo: Hannu Einarsson.

University library, Lund, 9.30 am. Enlightenment; while outside the thick stone walls, summer calls seductively. Lund University was founded in 1668 and has produced bountiful crops of geniuses and aesthetes. Swedish literary giants such as Frans G Bengtsson and Fritiof "Pirate" Nilsson studied here — when they weren't exhausted from drinking bouts, chess marathons and writing poetry. Even the best of students need occasionally to rinse their brains of French pronouns and historical battle dates. Photo: Per Lindström. *Next page.*

Frösön, Östersund, 6.32 am. Her name is Vilda (wild) and sometimes she's just that. But if there's a warm bottle of baby formula at hand, dad can snatch a little extra snooze-time. Mikael Larsson is on paid parental leave. Vilda is 16 months old, and very much a morning person. Photo: Pernilla Karström.

Stockholm's National City Park, 6.30 am.
Tuesday mornings, a crowd gathers at the nest. For fifteen years, Henrik Waldenström has guided groups of between 15 and 35 bird-watchers through the park's forests and lawns spotting both common and rare feathered friends. The amateur ornithologists are equipped with binoculars and tape recorders. Sparrow, you can run but you can't hide! Photo: Jan Delden.

Mälarhöjden School, Stockholm, 8.10 am.
Class 2A at Mälarhöjden School starts the day with a story. Teacher reads aloud, and the pupils can sit at their desks or lie on the floor. A lot of water has flowed under the bridge since Sweden's milestone school reform in 1842. It feels like light-years have passed since the days of wood-fired heating, psalm singing, inkwells, canes and banishment to the corner. Photo: Jan Lundberg. *Next page.*

Regimental exercise area, F10, Strängnäs, 0.32–9.03 am. At ease for a smoke. Twenty-year-old Per Glendor is training as platoon leader in an army that hasn't fired a shot in anger for almost two centuries. Swedish neutrality has survived two world wars and in recent years, the defence establishment has been slimmed down radically. Is it symbolic that the only smoke over the regimental exercise field is from a cigarette? Even in the tents, there's a lull in fighting. It's like a sauna in here and two conscripts are sleeping in their underpants. The conscript in charge of heating the tents did his job only too well. Photo: Frida Hedberg.

Mårtens väg road, Hjärup, 6.30 am. During the night, a hairy, heavy-breathing friend entered her bed. His name is Bertil and he is an enterprising whippet who has mastered the trick of sneaking in under mistress Monica Danielsson's bedclothes without waking her. After that, nothing disturbs them. Photo: Lars Brundin.

Höga Kusten Bridge, Ångermanälven River, 8.30 am. Construction engineers Frank Rosenberger and Thomas Neuman from the Alpin Technik company in Leipzig rappel down from the 178m-high pylon at the north end of the Höga Kusten Bridge. Not a job for the weak-nerved. Down below trucks whiz by like toys and even further down flows the Ångermanälven River, quietly and proudly. Photo: Erik G Svensson.

Järna, 11 am. "Bang, you're wet!" Hampus Johansson and Lucas Gustavsson are playing wet war games in the idyll of early summer in Sweden, far from the world's conflict spots. Photo: Matt Carey.

Årsta wholesalers' market, Stockholm, 4.30 am. What your arms can't carry, your mouth can. Johnny Leinmark woke up at half-past one to drive 60 km to Årsta market to buy fresh vegetables for his grocery store. He reckons the radishes are extra good. But balancing skill is needed to get the boxes to the car while simultaneously grabbing a quick morning coffee. And forget about yawning, despite the ungodly hour. Photo: Jan Delden.

Metro, Sundbyberg, 8.00 am. Free speech. Albert Taabu gives away copies of the free paper, Stockholm City—one of the pert new rags pumped out by newspaper publishers now also exploring cyberspace. Sweden's first daily newspaper was published in 1645 at the initiative of Chancellor Axel Oxenstierna and contained mostly letters from correspondents across Europe. More newspapers were published in Sweden in 1919 than any year before or since: 235 dailies. Today, there are 60 fewer, but we have new-fangled variations such as web papers, tele-text and advertisement-sponsored papers. Never has information been so copious, so swift—and so bewildering? Photo: Yvonne Åsell.

Drottninggatan street 73C, Stockholm, 7.10 am. Seventy-three-year-old Olle Eriksson has made his way down to the basement of his apartment building with a thermos of coffee and his clarinet — and suddenly, sweet music wafts through the narrow passageway under Drottninggatan 73C. Olle used to be a professional band musician, puffing away at wind instruments in the Royal Lifeguards Band and also a dance band. He loves music, but is aware that not all the neighbours share that love. Photo: Jack Mikrut. *Next page.*

Nolby and Skottsund, Sundsvall, 8.10 am–4.30 pm. Love every other day. Knut Sehlin is still living at home in Nolby village, not far from Sundsvall, but for the last seven years, his wife Birgit has been at an assisted-living home. Her legs won't carry her anymore and her eyesight has deterio–rated radically. Looking after her at home was too hard for Knut. Twenty-eight years ago, when they both turned 50, they gave each other a holiday in Thailand. They planned to live abroad six months of the year once they had retired. But their dream of a life in the tropics remained a dream. Knut's day is steered by the times he has to take his own insulin injections, but he can still cook his break-fast porridge, butter his bread and make sand–wiches to take to Birgit every second day. When they are together, they remember all the exciting people they've met and the places they've been. They both know that Birgit is never coming home again. In the upstairs bedroom at home, television is Knut's only company. Ever-inventive, he has worked out how to keep the strong sunlight at bay. Photo: Maria Eilertsen. *Also next spread.*

Maternity ward, General Hospital, Malmö, 10.30 am–12.20 pm. A new citizen arrives. Thomas Rakar and Anna Andersson were due for a cesarean operation hours ago, but then came the delays. Nervous giggling and gentle cuddling turned into frustration. And then, finally, the miracle: at 12.07 little Tilde was born — a little girl already equipped with easy confidence. Thomas slid into shock; he's a dad! Tears were followed by sudden clarity. It felt like nothing else existed but sweet little Tilde. In Sweden on the same day, 333 other babies were born. Photo: Emma Larsson.

Stockholm's Sjukhem nursing home, 10.30 am. Elly Söderqvist, 62, realises that her body is about to give up. Slowly, inexorably, life is draining away. For five months, she has been suffering from severe cardiac insufficiency. Treatment includes tactile massage for hands and feet, a kind of gentle touch technique that relaxes aching joints and provides some balm for the soul. The nursing home is not for those seeking a cure, just relief from pain as life slips away. Almost two months later, Elly's body finally surrendered. She died on 31 July. Photo: Jacob Forsell.

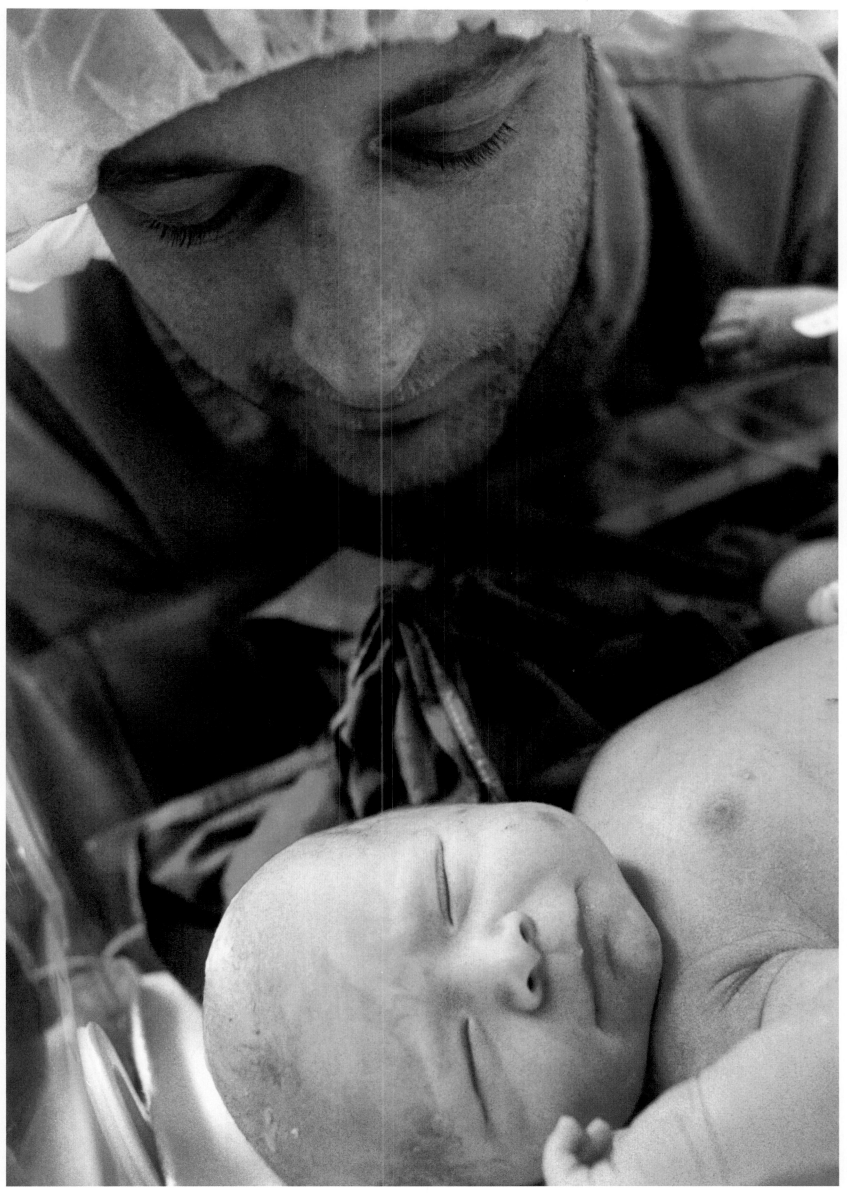

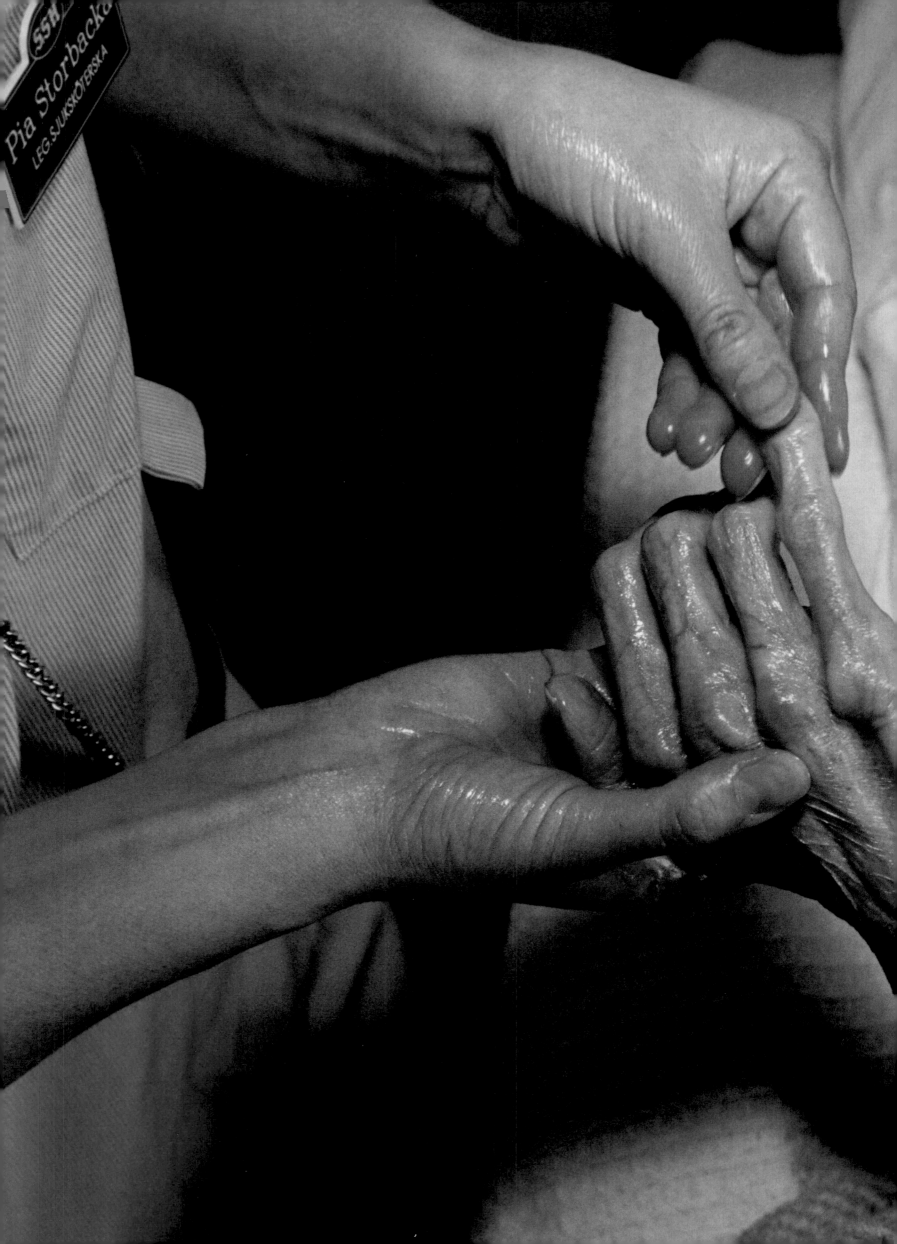

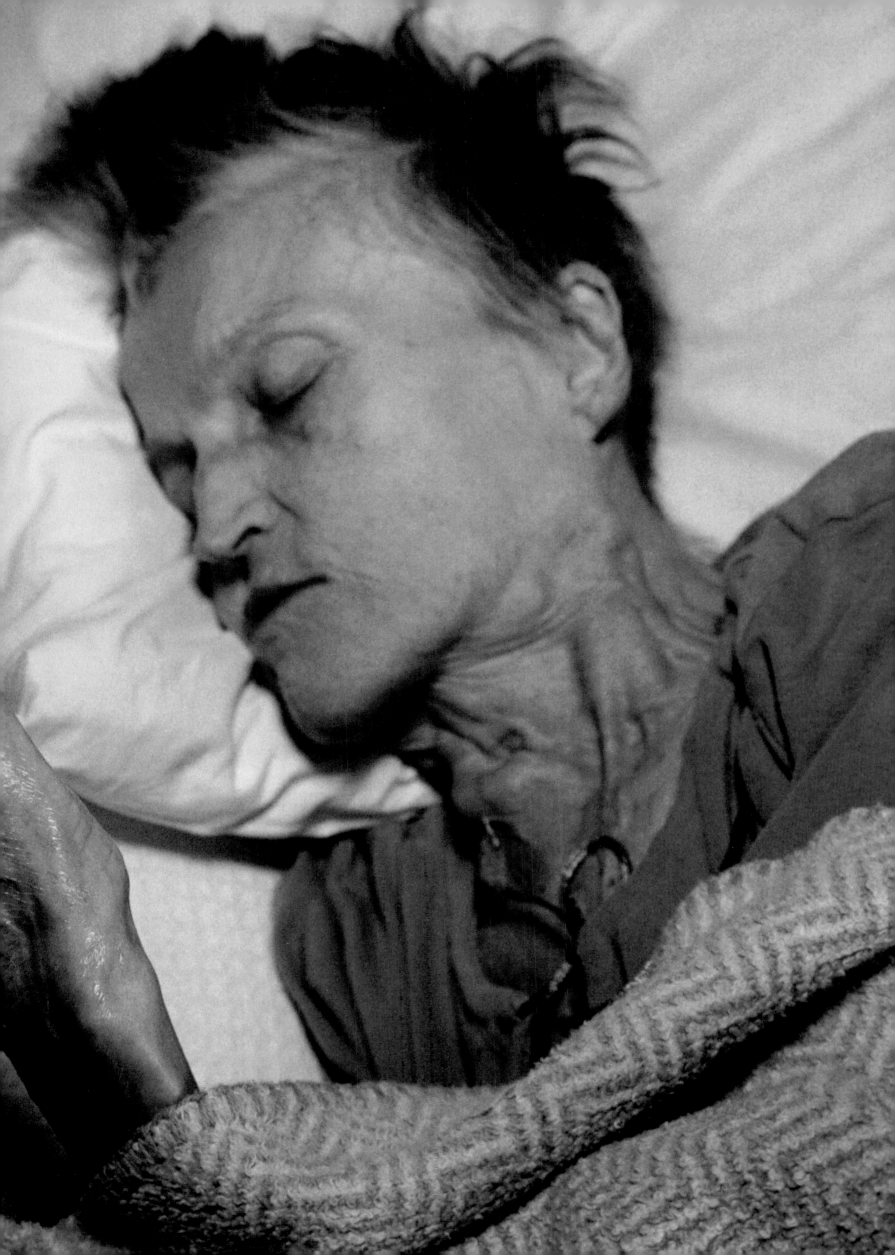

Överselö church, Stallarholmen, 12 noon. Brides of Christ, married to a life of prayer and contemplation. For 37 years, Sister Maj and Sister Ingrid have lived alone at the Convent of the Resurrection of the Lord outside Strängnäs. They have voluntarily abstained from marriage, children and worldly pleasures. Their life is tranquil, full of reflection and little chores. In Mikhail Bulgakov's classic novel "The Master and Margarita", the devil appeared in the disguise of a pitch-black cat. This animal is decidedly more pious; it answers to the name of Kimmie and is happy in the company of both nuns and God. Photo: Åke Ericson. *Previous page.*

Skivhugget record store, Andra Långgatan street, Göteborg, 11.50 am. "I'll take this one!" Fredrik Vieweg is overjoyed by the record store's huge inventory. He was about to buy a children's story about a cat's trip to America when he came across one of his favourite singers, Tomas Ledin. But Fredrik's carer Andreas Johansson points out that Fredrik already has that CD and anyway, he should lose his right to buy CDs if his taste in music doesn't improve. Underneath their posturing, there's a warm, intimate friendship. Andreas has been Fredrik's carer for two years. They are equally stubborn and quite fond of each other. Photo: Lisa Carlgren.

Brantevik, Österlen, southern Sweden, 11.30 am. Where would you find a better-ventilated barbershop than in Walter Huber's garden in Österlen, on the southern Baltic coast? Walter enjoys smartening up his friend Henry Johansson, roosted on a piano stool. "It's so beautiful outdoors, and you don't have to sweep up afterwards." Henry is no Samson; he's strong with or without his locks, and helps look after the garden in return for the haircut. And neither of them cuts corners. Photo: Bernt-Ola Falck.

Johannisberg campsite, Västerås, 11.35 am. He was a factory worker for 50 years. This is the first summer that Roine Eriksson doesn': have to reckon the days until he hears the pling of the time-clock again. Previously, he used his trailer only on weekends and holidays; now, it's every day. Often only for a cup of coffee or to lie in the sun and think. In Sweden, the state retirement pension was introduced in stages, but until 1948 retirees without savings still often depended on welfare handouts. Photo: Magnus Eriksson.

Northern Lapland, 10.40 am–4.05 pm. Half-way along the journey of her life, rural postal worker Mirja Niva finds herself on an obscure gravel track, far from civilisation's supermarkets and health centres. Every day, she covers 225 kilometres and visits 217 mailboxes on Sweden's northernmost public roads. Beyond the roadside ditch lurks wilderness. Swarms of mosquitoes splatter on her windscreen. Herds of reindeer often race across the road in front of her Volvo's bumper. "I've never had an accident, thank God. Sometimes I'll be driving for an hour without meeting another car. Winters are tough,obviously, with all that ice and snow. One January day in 1999 it was 53 Celsius below; I worked my route as usual." There's time for a quick coffee break with Hugo and Lily Eliasson in Närvä village (50 mailboxes), with freshly baked buns and some local gossip. A little further, in Idivuoma, tough, 90-year-old geezer Johannes Raatamaa has been waiting in the drizzle for the daily bounty of newspapers and advertising flyers. For most of her clients, Mirja Niva is the only link to the outside world, a welcome glimpse of light through the dark forest, a safety valve when the silence becomes too loud. As long as Mirja stays at her post, there is a modicum of social contact for the old and infirm. If letterboxes fill up, it's often a sign that something is not right. "I've been doing this for 15 years, ' says Mirja. "I can't imagine anything else. I like the solitude and putting the radio on loud and singing along." Photo: Björn Larsson Ask.

Österlen, 11.35 am–5.36 pm. A moment of inattention at the helm and black gold turns to deadly poison. Four days previously, the 225m bulk carrier Fu Shan Hai sank after colliding with a Cyprus-flagged Polish ship, the Gdynia. By Tuesday, the oil reached the coast of Skåne province, its coal-black, choking veil coating the beach, its sand and sea birds. Denied his morning dip, Almut Schacht turns back from his favourite beach with tears in his eyes. Further down the beach, clean-up is in progress: Wilhelm Boghammar from the local military garrison is spraying bark chips from a massive hose, while Johnny Berg from the Rescue Services is struggling in the heat with sticky black goo up to his elbows. A high price to pay for high living standards. Photos: Ola Fagerström (below), Jörgen Ahlström (right) and Linda Wikström (next page).

Kosta glassworks, 8.37 am–2.05 pm. Kosta, in the forests of Småland province, is Sweden's oldest manual glassworks, a sooty, fiery inferno where dull materials such as sand, potash and oxide turn into glittering, exquisite art. The glass mass is melted overnight in 1,430C-heat. When the glassblowers arrive at six in the morning, the glass is ready to be blown and shaped. His sweat glistening in the glow of the ovens, Master Glassblower Jan-Olof Augustsson is working on designs by Göran Wärf. This is a workplace where hierarchy is still deeply embedded and the nomenclature mysterious. Tattooed Bo Erlandsson, a 'Punty Sticker', adds the foot to wine glasses, while 'Bit Boy' Surapong Shaiwong fetches more glass mass from the oven. In an eight-hour session, they make 800 glasses. Kosta was founded in 1742, its name formed from those of the founders, regional governors Anders Koskull and Georg Bogislaus Staël von Holstein. Photo: Fredrik Funck. *Also next page.*

Keinovuopio, 3–6.30 pm. Seldom has nature been passed in a more beautiful setting than Europe's last wilderness. Little Jonas is visiting his uncle, Sixten Jensen, Sweden's northernmost inhabitant. His village, Keinovuopio, is 270km north of Kiruna, 30km from Treriksröset, where the borders of Sweden, Norway and Finland meet. To get there, Sixten has to drive over to Finland, park his car, strap on a backpack and trudge across a suspension bridge. Sixten gets occasional carpentry jobs in Norway, and his life is as international as for the bears, wolverines and lynx that wander back and forth across the national boundaries in Europe's last wilderness. Sixten's wife and mother also live in Keinovuopio. Today, they have visitors: a Norwegian friend, Kent Lundblad, and their nephew Jonas, who is eager to try out their new whitewater boat. The men work on the cabin they are building for tourists, with wood transported here across the ice last winter. Photo: Nicke Johansson. *Also previous page.*

Säve airport, 4 pm. Patrik Svantesson and Stefan Carlsson jump to it. They thrive on the vistas, the speed and the excitement. The duo is just passing 1,500m above sea level at a speed of 200kph. If those chutes fail to open, they will meet something hard in exactly 27 seconds… Photo: Anders Helgesson. *Next spread.*

Community Centre, Bjuv, 6.15 pm. Coffee and stakes. It's still two hours before bingo starts, but veteran players Nils Karlsson and Ruth Landgren have already reserved their favourite seats. "We moved here in 1969 and the first thing we found out about Bjuv was that the wrestling club had bingo evenings. So we skip afternoon coffee and cakes at home and have it here instead." For 40 years, the hall has echoed to the shout of 'Bingo!'

This is real bingo country; Sweden's first public bingo game was played in 1961 in Gunnarstorp, a stone's throw away. It's a cheap and popular pastime, most people agree. But over the last decade, bingo has burgeoned into a multi-million industry in Sweden, with a hugely popular TV show, Bingolotto, a major magnet. Stars such as David Bowie and the Pet Shop Boys appear on the show between bingo calls and players have won hundreds of thousands of euros.

Here in Bjuv, prize money is more modest and the entertainment consists of coffee breaks. Photo: Sven-Erik Svensson. *Previous page.*

Humlegården Park, Stockholm, 2.30 pm.
Grandma weeps tears of joy and mum thanks
a policeman for his help. In a matter of seconds,
a carefree sunny afternoon had become a drama.
In the park to play, three-year-old Raoul Ek had
managed to evade grandma's gaze just long
enough to disappear. Worry turned into anguish,
desperation and helplessness. Frantic, grandma
called Raoul's mother Judit and father Johan
Berggren to help search the park, but in vain.

At half-past one, they called the police. Several
units joined the search but after an hour had still
not found the three-year-old. Suddenly, there
he was, tightly hugging one of the tall trees in
front of the Royal Library at one end of the park.
Raoul had been told that if he ever gets lost in the
forest, not to rush around aimlessly but sit down
and hug a tree. But this time, the leaves and
vegetation were so thick that no one spotted the
little tree-hugger. Photo: P O Sännås.

Suburban Kålltorp, Göteborg, 5.01 pm.
"Hurray! A computer!" Andrea Tjäder is over the moon about her graduation present from the family. Around the table are grandmother Majken Nilsson, mother Kerstin Nilsson, cousin Henrik Nilsson, grandfather Arne Tjäder and great aunt Britt Nilsson. The best of all her schooldays is finally here. And the gravity of life is more real than ever. Photo: Anders Nilsson. *Previous page.*

Ornö, Vallentuna and Ingarö, 9.08 am–12.25 pm. He was cutting up wood with a power saw on Ornö island but got too close to the whirring blade. The ambulance helicopter was quickly on the spot and the doctor sees that four fingers are badly cut but are still attached. The 57-year-old man is in shock, but even with the pain and copious bleeding, realises it could have been worse. Similarly, the 23-year-old woman who crashed her messenger van outside Vallentuna complains about back pain but seems to have escaped with little more than shock. The third patient is a 56-year-old woman who fainted at home on Ingarö island and banged her head. All three places are in or close to Stockholm's

archipelago — it was principally to provide the islands with this kind of help that Sweden's and the world's first ambulance helicopter service began operations in 1948. When seas are surging, when the ice is close to bursting or melting, the helicopter is a last resort for medicine, stretchers and sound expertise. Nightsight glasses and radar allow the chopper to reach emergency cases even in hours of darkness. Many lives have been saved by the flying doctor of the islands. Photo: Lars Pehrson.

Görjansgården assisted-living residence, Ljusterö Island, 1.54 pm. Erik Fröberg says goodbye to his 94-year-old wife Vera, who is being taken by ambulance helicopter to a mainland hospital. Throughout life, the old couple has shared everything: joys, challenges and sorrows. Now they must part. Vera says her wrist is hurting and the doctor wants to take her to the hospital for X-rays. Vera shakes her head; she would rather stay and die with Erik. Her thin, bird-like body is strapped onto the stretcher and Erik says a quiet farewell before the helicopter takes off into the blue summer sky. "There you go, Vera — this is probably the last time we see each other," he mutters wearily and pats her sunken cheek with infinite gentleness and love. Five days later, Erik's lifetime partner is dead. Photo: Lars Pehrson.

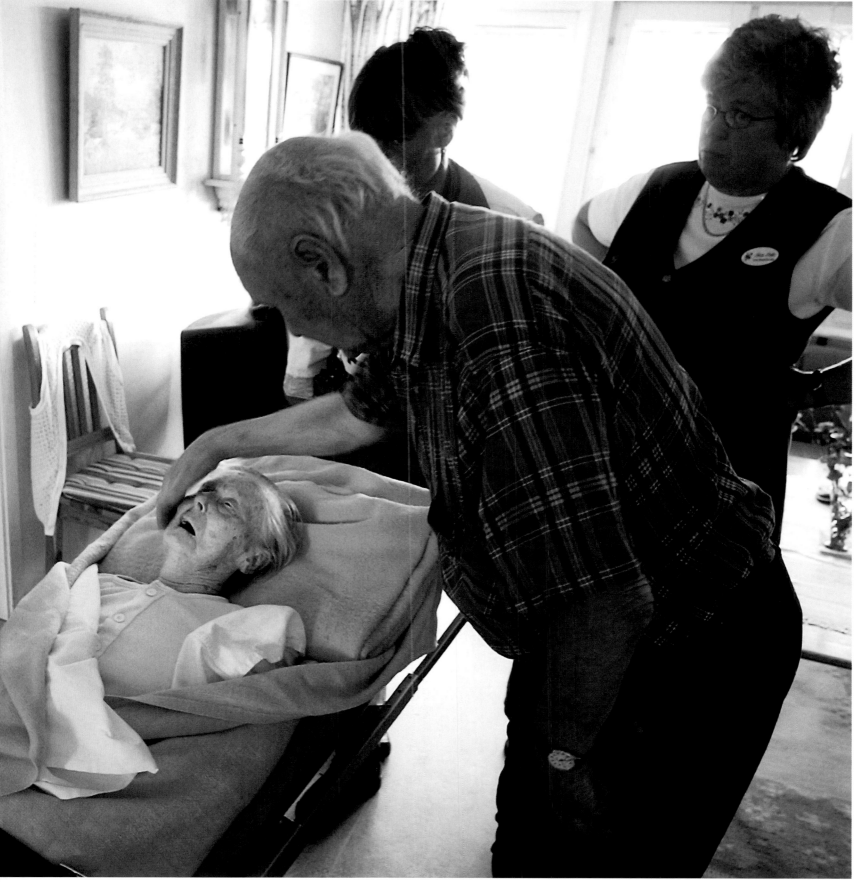

Sawadee Restaurant, Stockholm, 12.20 pm.
It's lunchtime again and chef Nui Kwandjanwad shifts into top gear behind her wok. The pace is brisk and the temperature high in the kitchen. Both the smells and the number of customers indicate that Sweden's basic foods are no longer pork sausage, mashed turnip, blood bread — hardly even potatoes. New immigrants have added to the menus and made them spicier, tastier and harder to pronounce. Without blinking, Swedes now gulp down everything from yakiniku to moussaka, rösti, tandoori, prosciutto and glass noodles: dishes previous generations had not even heard of. Much less knew how to prepare. Photo: Juki Nakamura.

Aspudden, Stockholm 1.39 pm. Her legs are not so supple anymore. But thanks to her walker frame and the local home-help service, Inga-Lisa does not have to give up her pleasant, airy apartment. Like many other seniors, she can take care of herself very well with only a little extra help. There has been immeasurable progress since the poorhouse days, less than a century ago. Photo: Ann-Sofi Rosenkvist.

The Astrid Lindgren Children's Hospital, Stockholm, 2.30 pm. He shouldn't even be able to play football, but he does. Erik Qvarner is in for a check-up after having a tumor taken from his right knee. Waiting for the doctor, he and his dad, Nils, have a kick-around in the corridor. They are both already dreaming about a return match, on grass and without the crutches. Photo: Roger Turesson.

Södertälje, 12.25 pm. Small blue men on a secret mission. Machine technicians at an Astra Zeneca facility are in an ad hoc meeting, perching on whatever they could find. Sweden's pharmaceuticals industry has built much of its wealth and success on research carried out in secret, well hidden from curious competitors' eyes. A new medicine might take ten years to produce for market. Astra had its major breakthrough in 1948 with Xylocaine, still the world's leading quick-acting local anaesthetic. Another winner has been Losec, a medicine for stomach ulcer conditions. Photo: Jack Mikrut. *Next page.*

Västra Ingelstad, 1.40 pm. Tracks of fear. A policeman checks the damage after a crash involving a train and a car on a crossing. The driver had just enough time to leap out before the train hit, and escaped with minor cuts to his face. A lone sandal is left under the twisted boom. Photo: Patrick Persson.

Somewhere in Sweden, 10.05 am–4.50 pm.
In the old story, Ahasverus the Wandering Jew was condemned to wander the world for centuries without ever finding a home and peace. The Osmanovic family with their ten children is the 21st-century equivalent of that reluctant nomad. They are stateless gipsies forced to move from country to country, jostled by authority all the while. Over the past eight years, the Osmanovics have lived in seven European countries. Their most recent hope was the oasis of Sweden,

rumoured to have a soft heart for the most oppressed. But even Swedish attitudes have hardened. And when the final notice of expulsion arrived, it was as though the walls had caved in. Tahira and Zaim's marriage has collapsed under the pressure, and Tahira has been rushed to hospital twice after attempts on her own life. Daily life is a slow, paralysingly uncertain process. But as if in protest, pictures are still hung on the walls, new dishes are cooked, pants are fixed and hope remains that

the family may one day live like any other, with jobs to go to and friends to invite home for dinner. Today, 3 June, the state of Sweden will register 187 new citizens, while more than 3,400 people are living like the Osmanovic family: illegally, in hiding, after having been formally notified of an expulsion order. They are Sweden's forgotten, hidden inhabitants. Photo: Joakim Roos. *Also next spread.*

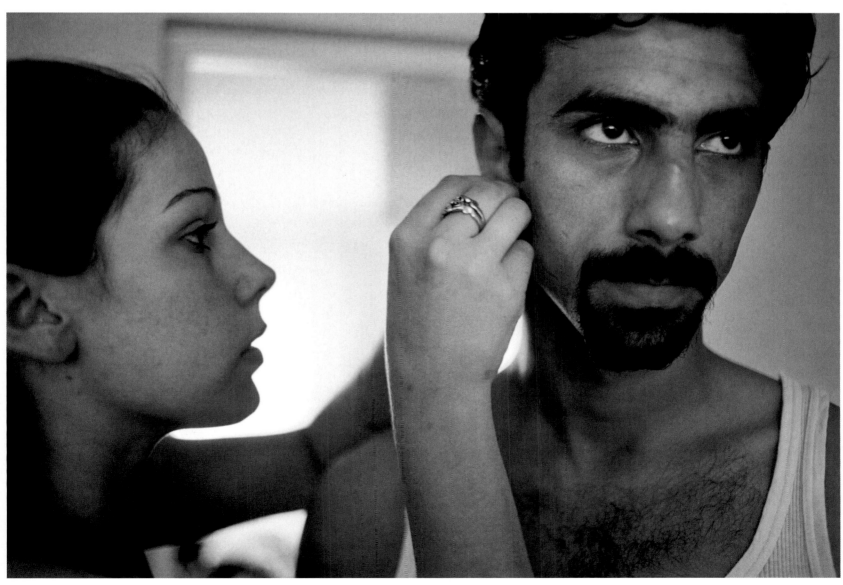

Seaside park, Malmö, 4 pm. The old lady has slowly emerged into the sun with the help of her walker frame and now two young guys are leaping towards her like kangaroos. Two worlds rubbing up against each other, two speeds, two cultures. We've all been kids, and yet not really in the same way. Growing up in Sweden in 2003 is completely different to growing up 60 or 70 years ago. The word 'teenager' was unknown until the 1950s. Photo: Henrik Saxgren.

Waterside promenade, Vadstena, 2 pm.
Sweden's second biggest lake, Lake Vättern, chops the province of Götaland in two. The water is deep — 128m in places — and hardly ever gets even slightly warm. But who cares about cold toes when summer is fresh and hot? Photo: Chris Maluszynski.

Fittja, 9.02 am–2.38 pm. One hundred and fifty children—and not one with a straight-arrow Swedish background. The Lightning Bug Day Care in Botkyrka, just south of Stockholm, is a glittering rainbow landscape of cultures and colours. Four-year-old Rozerin Barlas has spilt Swedish soured milk on her red dress at snack time. Melisa Varol is sulking because there's no seat for her on the carousel. Little Arvind Sritharan, whose parents are from Sri Lanka, gives a friend a hefty push before helping Cihan Yildrim hide behind a red mattress. Devran Özturk and Kajsa Toro, with a bench each, are having a private chat, still drowsy after their nap. Who gives a bean about skin colour or funny last names? Photo: Hanna Teleman. *Also next spread.*

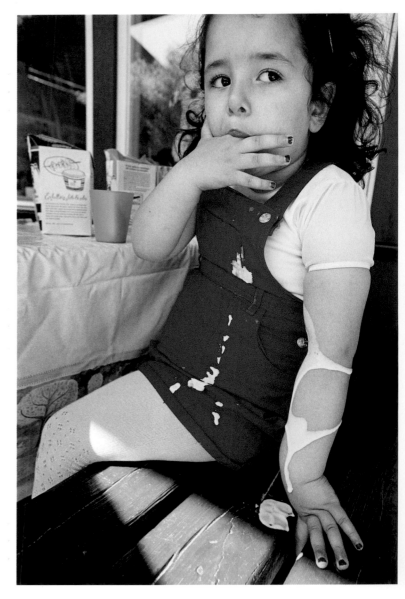

The Boat Day Care, Vaxholm, 1.30 pm. "All I want for Christmas is my two front teeth…" They'll be singing something like that later in the year at The Boat, a day care centre in the Stockholm archipelago. Of 19 kids in the section called The Raft, only six are still without that prestigious gap. Hanna is in first place with five missing pegs. Photo: Rolf Adlercreutz.

The trading room at SEB, Kungsträdgårds-gatan street, Stockholm, 2.35 pm. At the SEB bank's Trading Room, currency broker Anders Wickman juggles with millions of kronor. After the '90s made us all familiar with words like bull market, Porsche, liquidity and Wall Street puppie, the new millennium re-introduced concepts like bear market, bankruptcy, cut-backs and a growing under-class. Photo: Thomas Wågström.

Arlanda airport, Stockholm, 6.15 am–9.45 pm.
The first flight from here to New York took off in the spring of 1960. Primitive, shoebox terminals became a hypermodern airport with approximately 800 arrivals and departures and 55,000 passengers each day. Add 15,000 employees and Arlanda has more 'inhabitants' than some Swedish provinces. The parking area is the biggest north of Frankfurt. In many ways, Arlanda is its own universe with a multitude of professions, companies, dreams and goals. A young woman is killing time between flights and the Lidne family is waving off dad as he leaves for Venezuela. In the customs area, a man nervously scratches his head as two human sniffer dogs search his luggage. He's not sweating because he has done anything illegal but at the challenge of getting that suitcase shut again — he'd stuffed so many damn things in there. Photo: Pieter ten Hoopen.

Import Section, Malmö Harbour and Ribergsborg Baths, Malmö, 1.30–1.40 pm. From on high, we're all ants. Hundreds of Toyotas are waiting in Malmö harbour for transport to destinations throughout Scandinavia, while human beings tend their own chassis at the long-established bathing pavilions close by. Sweden's first car was a steamer built in 1892 by Jöns Cederholm. The Ribergsborg Baths, known as "Ribban", were erected on the shore of The Sound five years later by C H Richter, a walking-stick manufacturer who, legend has it, wanted someplace to wash his grubby son. Entrance was the equivalent of two cents and there was the added attraction of a café and a long-distance telephone. The bracing, 175m jog from the shore-line to the pavilions is now one of the pleasures of living in Malmö — a cleansing for body and soul. On hot days, the old plank floors are crammed with hundreds of near-naked bodies, but even on stormy winter evenings, you are liable to meet a few old enthusiasts, striding fearlessly through slushy snow to dive into the icy briny. Sweden has a total of 2,600 officially designated bading spots, on lakes or by the sea. Photo: Lars Bygdemark.

Stjärnsund, Dalarna province, 3.02 pm.
A timeless milieu — and at the same time, a workshop where you always know the time of day. A former farm-boy, Christopher Polhem (1661–1751) was a Renaissance man who achieved fame when he managed to repair the clock in the Uppsala Cathedral tower. In the early 18th century, Polhem also laid the foundations for Sweden's modern mining industry. And in addition to ingenious pump designs he created the classic Stiernsund Clock, a super-smart timepiece still being produced by clockmaker Robert Goude. The design has proudly stood the test of time for three centuries. Photo: Lars Dahlström.

The Yellow Room at SEB, Kungsträdgårds-
gatan street, Stockholm, 2.10 pm. Bank think
tank. In this cyber age, almost all transactions are
silent and invisible. The Swedish bank system
daily processes transactions worth hundreds of
millions of kronor, of which 99.9% is electronic
money. No rustling bank notes, no clinking coins.
The only shine in the Yellow Room comes from
the varnish on the imposing woodwork, as exe-
cutives participate in a tele-conference in English.
Photo: Lena Granefelt.

Krokshult, 2.50 pm. But in a farmhouse kitchen, you can still get by without credit cards. For years, small-holder Sture Caremalm has done all his sowing himself with a trusty work-horse, but today, he's just too tired. Neighbour Ivar Andersson says he will do the lot with his tractor for what amounts to small change. It's both relief and chagrin at the same time. Self-sufficiency is a thing of the past in Sweden, but in Krokshult, Sture's wife Britta can still spread a table with the farm's own produce: home-baked buns and biscuits, home-churned butter and her own cheese. Photo: Peter Gerdehag.

Air space above Läckö Castle, 1.35 pm. Hyper-modern technology meets cultural history when John "Jonte' Larsson and the fourth-generation Gripen fighter-bomber zoom by Läckö Castle. The JAS 39 Gripen was first built in 1988 and can reach a speed of Mach 2; it is one-third plastic, contains 30km of electric cable and has about 40 computers to run 450 different parts. Läckö Castle was built n 1298 on an island in Lake Vänern and is demonstrably far less susceptible to obsolescence. Photo: Major Ulf Fabiansson. *Next page.*

Alvhem, 12.45 pm. The chicken or the egg? In the grocery store in Alvhem village, there's no question about which comes first: Olle Larsson's eggs sell like hot cakes — customer orders are so constant that the eggs aren't even put on the shelves. The eggs are popular for omelettes, pancakes and hard- or soft-boiled breakfasts. Olle's hens are free-range creatures, raised on earthworms and tender loving care. Photo: Anna von Brömssen.

The Globe Arena, Stockholm, 4.10 pm. The pews in Swedish churches may be empty, but a drained ice hockey rink collects 12,000 Swedes to listen to a bald man talk religion and politics. There is a rock star feel to the Dalai Lama, or Tenzin Gyatso as he was originally named. According to Tibetan belief, he is a Bodhisattva: an enlightened being who chose to delay his departure for Nirvana and instead be reborn again and again to serve humanity. This is his fourteenth life, he says. No wonder the Globe is sold out. But Tenzin Gyatso's holy status apparently has no influence on the common cold; he is not well and excuses himself to cough several times during his speech. This apostle of peace also reveals that he was not especially well-behaved as a child: "I used to scratch my brother with my nails!" Photo: Jan Collsiöö.

Mälarhöjden, Stockholm, 6.15 pm. A suburban Bhudda relaxes behind the venetian blinds. It has been a hectic day. The great Dalai Lama has appeared at the Globe Arena and one of his lesser-known brethren Lama Ngawang was naturally there to listen to the wisdom. Lama Ngawang came to the cold North 30 years ago to spread the teachings of another enlightened man, Siddharta Gautama. Lama Ngawang settled down in the lotus position in a little house in the Stockholm suburb of Mälarhöjden and has open house for like-minded souls every Tuesday and Thursday at six. From outside, his home is a standard brown wooden house, no stand-out on the street. Inside, it is a piece of Tibet in exile, known by the tongue-twisting name Karme Shedrup Dargye Ling. Photo: Claes Löfgren.

Micro-technology Centre, Chalmers University of Technology, Göteborg, 2.30 pm. It's all in the detail. At Section MC2 at the Swedish stronghold of technology, Chalmers University of Technology, Philippe Komissinski knows this is true in more than one way. The section produces tiny laser cannons and microchips in a meticulous process of fine-tuning that demands rigorous method and orderliness throughout. Nano technology is utterly dependent on clean surfaces free from alien particles and disruptive vibration. For symbol buffs, there is much to glean from the rows of latex gloves hanging among chemicals of mysterious origin. This represents the intrusion of a new industrial economy into a micro-cosmos a world apart from classic industry milieu such as roaring steelworks and paper factories. Photo: Peter Magnusson.

Karolinska Institute, Stockholm, 4 pm. Sparkling, beautiful — and deadly. The first picture of the SARS virus — yet another deadly acronym to add to our recent catalogue. This virus was taken from a German man who contracted it in Asia. It was flown under the strictest security to Stockholm where it was neutralized using glutaraldehyde in a security level 3 laboratory, the second highest. It takes only 15 minutes for the virus to force entry to a cell. After six hours, infection is a fact and many cells have already been given the kiss of death. Plague is a fearful foe, whether it comes in the guise of SARS, Aids or Ebola, but thanks to the electron microscope's ability to magnify a quarter of a million times, we at least know the cut of its armour. Perhaps to find a chink in it? Photo: Lennart Nilsson.

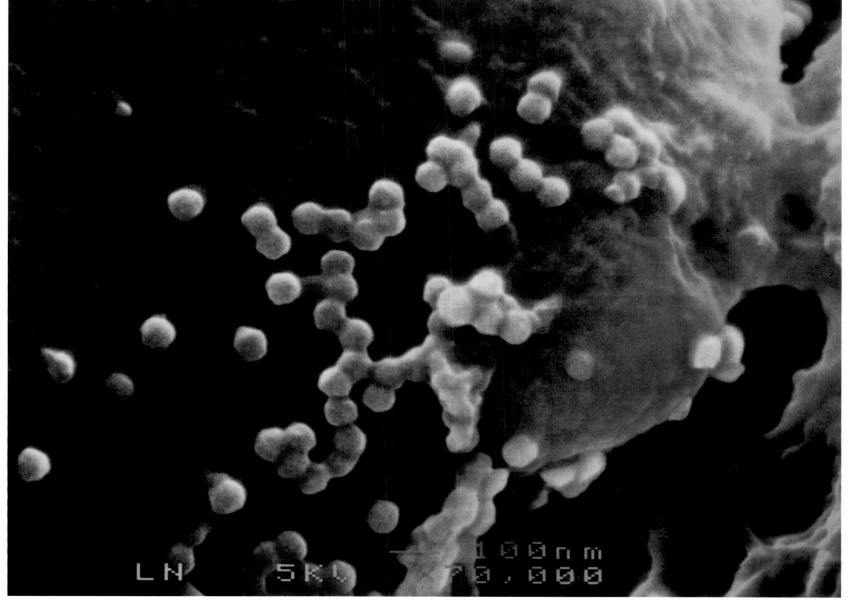

Cableway, Åre, 6.20 pm. Patrik Svärd and Ulf Andersson grease support cables on the almost century-old cableway up to the 1,420m peak of Åreskutan. The ski season is over, the valley lies green below and the potentially dangerous maintenance work begins. Photo: Thomas Dahlberg.

West Harbour, Malmö, 4.25 pm. A leap into the water—and into the future. They've come on their bikes to the canal for a refreshing swim after school. The children from immigrant-dense Rosengård district are the new Swedes, with both unique opportunities and a steeper hill to climb than others. Rosengård has a mixed variety of cultures, aromatic food, and Sweden's newest soccer star, Zlatan Ibrahimovic — but also crime, alienation and a leaden, fearsome unemployment. Will these be gangstas or happy bathers? Photo: Torbjörn Andersson.

Central Station, Stockholm, 2.30–5.18 pm.
A man gets off a train, another gets on. Stockholm Central is the heart of the circulatory system that is the Swedish transport infrastructure. This is where Swedes change direction, stop and accelerate. In rush hour, there is a palpable increase in pulse, stress, crush and wrong turns. For many, trains are a symbol of freedom, leave-taking, and endless adventure. For others, they represent mostly everyday, monotonous commuting on sticky seats behind fogged-up windows. Photo: Daniel Roos.

Downtown Malmö, 3.10 pm. "But I was just…" Swedes are polite people who rarely raise their voices. But not when parking fines are concerned. Seldom are they so angry, so livid, so utterly infuriated over society's injustices as when they discover that oblong white ticket pinned under a windscreen wiper. And it can actually pay off to argue back. Richard Lindberg spent 20 minutes in animated discussion with parking attendants Efsatathios Notou and Kent Persson — and was let off a parking fine. Photo: Torbjörn Andersson.

Gunnebo Lifting Company, Småland province, 1.03–4 pm. The entire town is nailed down. Little Gunnebo with its 1,200 inhabitants lives and breathes with its factory, a giant redbrick plant. The first nail produced by the company was forged in 1764. Today, production has been spun off into divisions for different specialities such as nails, fencing and chains. Recent decades have been cruel ones for Sweden's small, factory-based communities. It is barely a generation since almost all Gunnebo kids had a father who worked behind those rugged iron gates. Today, Bosse Öhr is one of the few who still have access to the shower room to wash away the day's dust. Ulf Johansson and Hasse Åkesson are cycling back to their work-stations after lunch at the canteen. Perhaps symbolically, the factory clock doesn't show the correct time. In Gunnebo, they still dream about the old times. Photo: Magnus Pettersson.

Hamngatan street, Stockholm, 2.18 pm. "Have a nice day!" Six-year-old Fredrik Johansen is indifferent to the American hamburger giant's charm. Once upon a time, junk food in Sweden was synonymous with greyish frankfurters swimming in greasy water at the outdoor dance or the sports arena. Today, food in Sweden is cosmopolitan, both up-market and down-market. Hamburgers go under various names: Max, Mc, Big or Mamma Scan. And if you ask for a sausage today, you'd better define whether it's chorizo, salami, home-grown isterband, medister veal sausage, Polish beer sausage or German knack-wurst. Photo: Anette Nantell.

Shopping centre, Smålandsstenar, 12.34 pm. Margit Andersson relaxes with a glass of cordial and a gossip magazine in her own special spot, hard by the parking lot. She claims not to hear the cars any longer. Heavy traffic thunders along a highway 30m away, but there's peace and tranquillity in Margit's little space with the yellow curtains and red geraniums. At times, paradise can be tucked away behind a blue Volvo. Photo: Hannu Eirarsson.

Krokshult, 12.35–6.10 pm. The cows' last summer. Inez Wigren has already chosen which two of her milk cows will first go for slaughter. She trudges down the old village road, glancing at the old farm tree and remembering when people had the strength and means to run small farms in Sweden. Today, if you're not on a large holding, it's tough going. No one can make a living from only six cows, but Inez is determined to continue, putting more effort into sheep. "They keep the landscape in trim." Over by the tilled field, the thirst break is over and brothers Karl-Uno and Sture Caremalm sit watching their neighbour Ivar Andersson start his tractor to sow the last patch with barley. The bag has been in service since the Sixties Photo: Peter Gerdehag.

Ribersborg bathing house, Malmö, 4.15 pm. Café au naturel. Ulla Wulff has brought her thermos and a good book with her to the sun deck; Maj-Britt Ramshög carries her clothes to the locker room. Nowhere is the sun worshipped so lovingly as in the frosty, mountainous North. For almost nine months, Swedes are introverted, reserved souls, crouching in front of the TV while snow and ice pile up against the triple glazing. But under thick layers of wool and Goretex is hidden a more open and relaxed individual. Photo: Anette Eriksson. *Next page.*

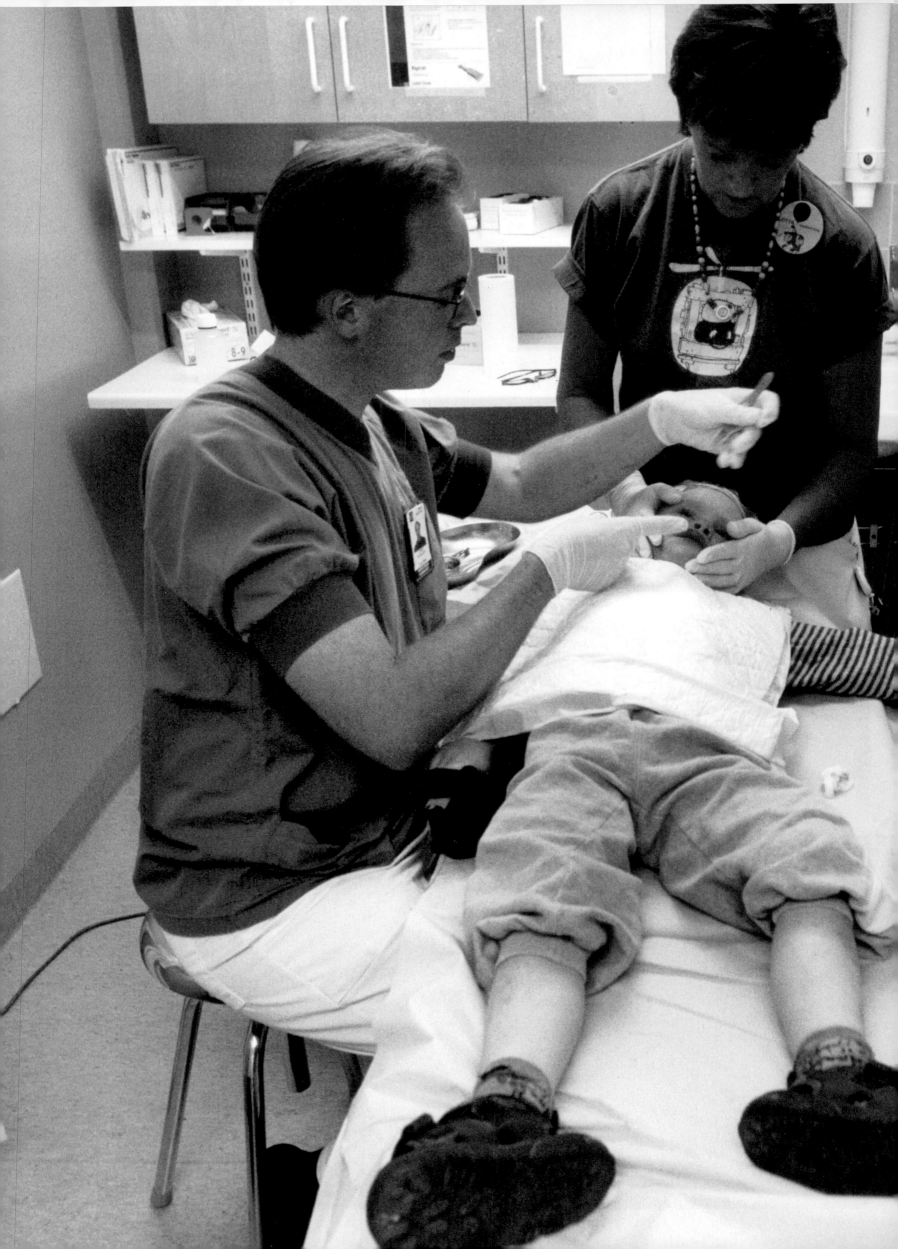

Emergency ward, Astrid Lindgren's Children's Hospital, Stockholm, 10.20 pm. Jacob Wahlström was on his bike when he bumped into his big brother, hit the road and burst his lip. Mother Carin has had a tough evening with lots of worry and little food. When Dr. Johan Danielsson began to stitch Jacob's lip, Carin got weak at the knees and had to lie down, a hospital blanket under her head. "Emergency ward visits are often harder on the parents than the children," comforts nurse Lotta Karlsson. "But it's more often the dads who faint." Photo: Roger Turesson.

Vadstena Abbey, Vadstena, 3–8.30 pm. It's a birthday party for a tough, 700-year-old lady and everybody wants to take home a memory. St. Birgitta (1303-1373) was a mother of eight who authored prayers, scolded kings, travelled to Rome and became one of the most prominent political lobbyists of the 14th century. Seven centuries later, she is still amazingly living. This is her anniversary year and her grey-clad brothers and sisters have travelled from across the world to Vadstena to hold conferences, exchange thoughts, take pictures and recite her prayer: "Show me, Lord, Your path and give me the will to take it." When a chest containing her relics is opened for public display — a rare and solemn occasion — there is commotion at the altar. Hundreds of demure nuns suddenly become excited school children with itchy fingers. It is hard to keep from stroking the bone remains or at least touching them with rosary beads. Photo: Chris Maluszynski. *Also previous page.*

City Park, Jönköping, 7.38 pm. As the accordion crushes mosquitoes, sweat rises in armpits and permanent waves. It's fun night in the classic Dance Pavilion in the park, and every floorboard has its robber sheikh and kidnapped princess. Afterwards, there'll be coffee and cookies and soggy napkins. The craze for 'lite' dance music — in Sweden, a country music hybrid run on syrup instead of excitement — has always had geographically patchy acceptance. Its spiritual home is the deep forest country around Värmland province, with another vein running through the picturesque dales of southern Småland and Blekinge provinces. All over, dreams are woven and unravelled in 2/4 time. When the summer sky slowly darkens, both dancers and mosquitoes become more purposeful. Photo: Hannu Einarsson.

Morastrand, Mora, 10.32 pm. To the junk yard or the party? Hanna Hansback and Sara Forsgren have borrowed a car for the traditional cortege through town when friends of theirs graduate from school the next day. Rusty holes have been rubber-cemented and the grille bravely duct-taped together. The registration plate has seen better days, too. But the car actually passed its latest roadworthiness test with flying colours. Photo: Pasi Autio.

Norrskedika sports ground, 7.08 pm. No, he didn't get a chance to blast his signal horn this time. Nisse Grönlund has travelled 70km with Lord, his boxer, for a drive-in bingo. It turned out to be a quiet evening; far too quiet. According to some authorities, the word 'bingo' comes from 'bing', the sound made by the gong that used to be struck when someone had a winning set of numbers. If Nisse had been around then, the game might well have become known as 'beepo'. Photo: Peter Lydén.

Castle Park, Halmstad, 7.08 pm. On a patch of grass in Halmstad, southern Sweden, a gang of summer-time skiers still hasn't noticed the skis are missing. Hiking poles have quickly won followers in Sweden, not least among feisty seniors. It's cross-country skiing and modern gymnastics in the same movement, say enthusiasts. There are more and more fans — and fitter than ever. Photo: Anders Andersson.

Wasa sports centre, Södertälje, 6.37 pm.
She may be heir to the throne, but on the floorball court others rule. Crown Princess Victoria
Ingrid Alice Desirée gets up-close and rough
with Daniel Åsbrink, captain of the Telge Vikings,
and gets a lesson in the difficult art of wheel-
chair floorball. The club is one of many given
donations from the Crown Princess's Fund.
Photo: Magnus Grimstedt.

Guldheden, Göteborg, 6.17 pm. The world's best toy is in motion in the tiniest village and the greyest concrete ghetto. Sweden's first football match was played in Göteborg. The pioneer clubs were the Soldiers of Fortune, founded in 1883 and Örgryte Sports Association, 1887, with a playing staff composed mainly of immigrant Scots from the curtain factory. In 2003, hundreds of kids are still out there on Guldheden's gravel pitch, still dreaming of fame as professionals. On this field of dreams, it's World Cup final every evening. Photo: Niklas Larsson.

Hagaström sports ground, Gävle, 8.09 pm.
"OK, guys, let's get 'em!" The official match
timekeeper starts the clock for the second half
in a fourth division soccer match pitting local
lads Hagaström against Valbo. There are 75
spectators in the stands. The final score is 1–1.
We're a long, long way from San Siro and
Wembley. Photo: Jenny Lundberg.

Sahlin's ostrich farm, Borlänge, 7.20 pm. Stick at the ready, Gunnar Sahlin keeps the largest males at bay for the evening egg collection. Ostriches have a kick like a horse and razor-sharp claws; there are horror stories about people having their stomachs split open by a single kick. The ostrich's natural habitat is the African savannah, but in recent years, they have become an increasingly less exotic sight in the Swedish countryside. As traditional farms fail, country people are being forced to find new sources of income, new products. For those unwilling to just bury their heads in the sand, there is always a way. Photo: Henrik Hansson.

City Park, Jönköping, 7.27 pm. "Yes!" Even if you'll never be another Annika Sörenstam, it's always great to sink a hole-in-one. On the other hand, Swedish columnist Cello once noted: "Life is like a golf ball. You get hit around a lot. Then wind up in a hole in the ground." Photo: Hannu Einarsson. *Next page.*

North of Falkenberg, 6.33 pm. She doesn't appreciate being beached. While mother Linnea, 27, tries to change, seven-week-old Vampira gets all upset in her baby carrier. Pontus the dog, 14, is tired of little missy's ways and indicates impatiently that he's ready to go home. Photo: Niklas Henrikczon.

E-18 House, Västerås, 6–9 pm. Ever wondered where Death Lobby is? It's in a ramshackle house right by highway E-18 in Västerås. Punk was born in 1976 as an anarchistic protest against the establishment, consumerism and — perhaps not least — the more decorous music preferred by that generation of parents. In Sweden, several band names became legendary: The Pig Screams, Garbo Shock, Anal Sweat… At E-18 House, protest lives, in beaming health and at eardrum-piercing volume. Youth recreation centres have been closing one after the other for lack of funds, but music still blares from these windows, drowning out the roar of traffic. Death Lobby consists of Jenny Wallén on bass, Fredrik Karlsson on guitar, Fredrik Hulterström on drums and Magnus Larsen and Magnus Welander, vocals. Photo: Marta El-Masri.

Enskede sports ground, Stockholm, 6.50 pm.
Are these the hope of the future? Our next stars?
Nine year-olds Julia Carls, Nellie Kullman and
Amanda Lindgren zoom over the final hurdle as
Hammarby sports club's youngest athletes train
speed and fitness. The girls are old friends, and
train together once a week. There's still lots of
playing and giggling on the red track, but there
is also a vague dream of fame and accomplish-
ment. Photo: Jack Mikrut.

Hard Rock Café, Stockholm, 9.30 pm. Please release me… Heavy metal rockers Stormwind are releasing their sixth album, "Rising Symphony", and are celebrating with a rambunctiously with decibels, drinks and distortion. On the other hand, what was it those famous rock fakes Spinal Tap said? "If there's sex and drugs, who needs rock'n'roll?" Photo: Jonas Lund.

Spånga, Stockholm, 7.45 pm . A clever little predator gets her reward. Eleven-year-old Jenny Larsson is a member of Owl Patrol in the local scout troop, and tonight badges are awarded as the term ends. It's a big day for a little pathfinder. As a Swedish scout, she is part of a worldwide youth movement with 25 million members in 150 countries. In 1907, Robert Baden-Powell started his outdoor adventure movement based partly on laws used by the knights of the Middle Ages regarding honesty, courage, honour and selflessness. Ninety-six years later, there are still those who are constantly prepared. Photo: Claes Löfgren

Katrineholm, 8.46 pm. "Who's that stamping on my bridge?" Lotta Culmsee reads to her four-year-old daughter Ebba. It's a classic Norwegian children's story about three goats and a bad troll. Ebba holds her breath: hungry trolls are both fun and kind of spooky at bedtime. Photo: Roger Culmsee.

Sunne farm, Vike, 8.15 pm. Back to the land. On the Pettersson farm, 50km from Sundsvall, farmer's daughter Anna Hjerpe swabs down the teats of Elin-217 before evening milking. Elin has 415,000 milky sisters across the country, nearly a quarter of a million fewer than 20 years ago. The fields where once Sweden's emigrants to America cleared stone to plant crops are now being taken over by forest. Shepherd boys have become meat factory managers. Only a fraction of Sweden's population — 160,000 persons — try to make a living from the profession that has provided work for a vast majority over the last thousand years. Photo: Bodil Bergqvist.

Lygna hamnskär, Stockholm archipelago, 8.23 pm. All day long they have been checking fishing nets, gutting fish, collecting down and emptying the outhouse. Time to relax with a glass of wine or two beside a cottage wall bathed in soft evening sunlight. Magdalena Rinaldo has invited Roland Olsson and Maria Kjellström to one of the archipelago's small homes to put civi-lisation on hold a while. The only sounds are the lapping of the waves and the seabirds. Photo: Staffan Widstrand. *Next spread.*

Royal Opera, Stockholm, 11.48 am–8.04 pm.
When she was little, she used to race around
flapping her arms, playing butterflies or ghosts.
Now, Nathalie Nordquist is one of the Royal
Opera's five solo dancers, a 24-year-old prima
ballerina now facing her greatest role, as Aurora
in Sleeping Beauty. It's a childhood dream come
true: a dance on tiptoe through make-up boxes
and tutus—but also through sweat, struggle and
wear and tear. A night at the opera is seldom all
roses. It's a tough, lonely and rather unglamorous
job that grinds down body and soul. A career in
dancing is short and similar to an athlete's. In a
one-hour 'class', Nathalie does approximately
1,000 tendues or leg stretches, and so far in her
career has worn out 184 toe shoes, which is com-
paratively few. When muscles shriek in protest,
physiotherapist Jane Salier-Eriksson comes to
the rescue. In the quiet minutes before a perfor-
mance, Nathalie consolidates her strength and
inspiration among the closets, running to the
bathroom now and then and attempting to master the butterflies in her stomach. Curtain up!
Photo: Anette Nantell. *Also next page.*

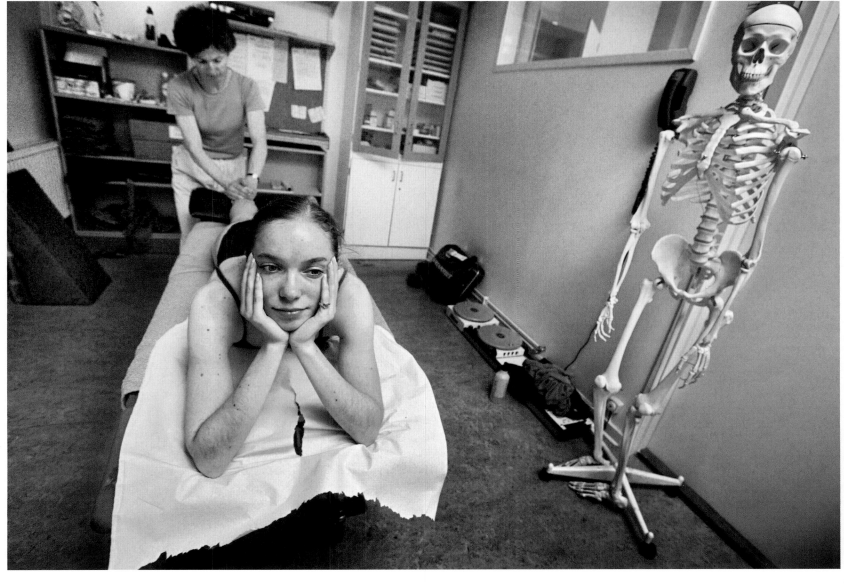

PHOTO INDEX

THANK YOU

Bokförlaget Max Ström extends its grateful thanks to all those who contributed to A Day in the Life of Sweden.

Päivi Aaltonen
Mark Abbawi
Björn Abelin
Fredrik Abrahamsson
Richard Abrahamsson
Sofie Abrahamsson
Dilman Abu Bakr
Mikael Ackelman
Rolf Adlercreutz
Jonas Adolfsson
Patrik Adolfsson
Åsa Adolfsson
Mats Adsten
Aida Adzemovic
Per-Anders Agdler
Rune Agdler
Fredrik Ahl
Boel Ahlandsberg
Johan Ahlberg
Linnéa Ahlberg
Maria Ahlberg
Sten Ahlberg
Tomas Ahlberg
Maria Ahlby
Henrik Ahlén
Joakim Ahlén
Karel Ahlfort
Karolina Ahlfort
Conny Ahlgren
Sture Ahlgren
Emma Ahlin
Erik Ahlin
Ewa Ahlin
Mikael Ahlin
Eva Ahlin-Jonasson
Christer Ahlm
Camilla Ahlnäs
Janina Ahlqvist
Daniel Ahlstedt
Fredrik Ahlström
Jörgen Ahlström
Jessica Ahrling
Petra Ahston Inkapööl
William Aimard-Camus
Stephanie Aimard-Camus
Jan Ainali
Eila Akkila
Krister Aktiv
Eduardo Alaye
Stig Albansson

Eva Alberts
Emil Albihn Henricsson
Niclas Albinsson
Anders Aldberg
Jens Alén
Mattias Alenljung
Martin Alexandersson
Martin Alfredsson
Michael Alfredsson
Silvia Ali
Bengt Allebrink
Jan Allenby
Patrik Allgulander
Anders Alm
Erik Alm
Jessica Alm
Kristian Alm
Mats Alm
Per Olof Alm
Thorsten Alm
Johan Almén
Berit Almér
Johan Almers
Malin Almers
Susanne Almers
Eva Almgren
Jan Almlöf
Curt Almqvist
Gunilla Almroth
Kjell Alpmo
Annika Alsén
Miriam Alster
Mats Althin
Rodrigo Alvarado
Elisabeth Alvenby
Klas Haralambos
    Amanatiadis
Miki Anagrius
Annie Anderberg
Eirin Anderberg
Lars Anderberg
Olle Anderby
Maj-Lis Andersén
Christopher Anderson
Anders Andersson
Andreas Andersson
Anneli Andersson
Arne Andersson
Björn Andersson
Bo Andersson

Bo-Lennart Andersson
Camilla Andersson
Carina Andersson
Christer Andersson
Christian Anderssson
Dag Andersson
Daniel Andersson
Emma Andersson
Erik Andersson
Erik A Andersson
Eva Andersson
Eva-Lotta Andersson
Ewa-Lena Andersson
Gunilla Andersson
Göran Andersson
Hans Andersson
Heike Andersson
Henry Andersson
Håkan Andersson
Ingela Andersson
Isabelle Andersson
Jan Andersson
Jenny Andersson
Jens Andersson
Jessica Andersson
Johan Andersson
Jonas Andersson
Jörgen Andersson
Katja Andersson
Kerstin Andersson
Kjell Andersson
Klas Andersson
Kristina Andersson
Lars Andersson
Leif Å Andersson
Lillemor Andersson
Linda Andersson
Lotten Andersson
Louise Andersson
Magnus Andersson
Malin Andersson
Maria Andersson
Marie Andersson
Markus Andersson
Mats Andersson
Mia Andersson
Mikael Andersson
Mikaela Andersson
Mårten Andersson
Niklas Andersson

Per Andersson
Per-Olof Göran
    Andersson
Ralf Andersson
Robert Andersson
Robin Andersson
Rolf Andersson
Rosalie Andersson
Sanna Andersson
Stefan Andersson
Susanne Andersson
Sylve Andersson
Therese Andersson
Tobba Andersson
Tobias Andersson
Tommy Andersson
Torbjörn Andersson
Torunn Andersson
Tove Andersson
Ulrika Andersson
Urban Andersson
Victor Andersson
Viveca Andersson
Åke Andersson
Erik André
Anna Andreasson
Bengt Andreasson
Martin Andreasson
Mats Andreasson
Inge Andréasson
Ann Andrén
Björn Andrén
Claes Andrén
Gunnar Andrén
Jacob Andrén
Kjell Andrén
Jan Andresen
Dragi Anevski
Lennart Anglemar
Peter Angvarson
Anders Anjou
Sophie Ankreus
Johan Annerstedt
Mats Ansén
Petter Antonisen
Frida Antonson
Ingegerd Antonsson
Rolf Antonsson
Lotta Appelgren
Björn Appelqvist

Magnus Ardeby
Mattias Ardvik
Stefan Areving
Jens Arfvelin
Lisa Arfwidson
Arto Argutin
Jan Arleklint
Fredrik Armstrand
Moa Arnberg
Lars Arned
Malin Arnesson
Peppe Arninge
Olle Aronsson
Göran Arontzon
Krista Arplund
Sven Arrelöv
Bo Arrhed
Casimir Artmann
Staffan Arvegård
Martin Arvidson
Gun-Inger Lorentzdotter
    Arvidsson
Hans Arvidsson
Johan Arvidsson
Kenneth Arvidsson
Stefan Arvidsson
Joakim Arwidson
Sanna Arwidsson
Mia Askerlund
Ingamay Askestad
Kerstin Asp
Eva Aspling
Emelie Asplund
Kalle Assbring
Georgios Athanasiadis
Monica Atterberg-
    Göransson
Peter Atterfjäll
Marie-Louise Atterhag
Anders Attermark
August
Maria Augustsson
Kristjan Aunver
Pasi Autio
Gidon Avraham
Arne Axelsson
Bengt Axelsson
Bo Axelsson
Hanna Axelsson
Kristin Axelsson

Lars Axelsson
Nils Axelsson
Peter Axelsson
Åke Axelsson
Lisa Bacharach
Eric Back
Jonas Backlund
Annika Backman
Sofia Bäckman
Birgit Bäck-Persson
John Bäckstrand
Hanna Bäckström
Marcus Bäckström
Ralf Bäckvik
Ruben Badager
Leif Baggström
Peter Bahrke
Julia Bakall
Andrew Bakama
Jessica Balac
Claudia Balboa
Mehdi Barakat
Pawel Baranczewski
Tiberius Tibor
    Transylvanicus Barany
Mattias Bardå
Andreas Bardell
Göran Bardun
Brigitte Barenfeld
Christian Barenkob
Inga Bark
Peter Barklund
Peter Bauer
Uwe Behrens
Roland Beijer
Lisa Bekkouche
Martin Belak
Andreas Belanner
Marie Bendegard
Sara Bender
Szilard Benedek
Arne Bengtsson
Bjorn Bengtsson
Elenor Bengtsson
Gustav Bengtsson
Håkan Bengtsson
Kenneth Bengtsson
Leif Bengtsson
Lennart Bengtsson
Lotta Bengtsson

Malena Bengtsson
Mattias Bengtsson
Mikael Bengtsson
Niklas Bengtsson
Per-Elof Bengtsson
Pär Bengtsson
Roland Bengtsson
Åse Bengtsson
Marcus Bennäs
Pauline Benthede
Anna Berg
Ingegerd Berg
Maria Berg
Micke Berg
Patric Berg
Solveig Berg
Tomas Berg
Maria Bergara
Elin Berge
Mikael Bergerholm
Clas Berggren
Jonas Berggren
Michael Berggren
Svante Berggren
Johan Berglin
Per-Erik Berglin
Ann-Britt Berglund
Dan Berglund
Maria Berglund
Nils Berglund
Peter Berglund
Stephan Berglund
Thomas Berglund
Ulf Berglund
Ulla-Britt Berglund
Anna Bergman
Annie Bergman
Björn Bergman
Magnus Bergman
Peter Bergman
Rose-Marie Bergman
Tomas Bergman
Johan Bergmark
Peter Bergmark
Anders Bergqvist
Bodil Bergqvist
Gunilla Bergqvist
Göran Bergqvist
Irene Bergqvist
Martin Bergqvist
Olof Bergqvist
Anna Bergsten
David Bergström
Ingrid Bergström
Jonas Bergström
Katharina Bergström
Magnus Bergström
Per-Olof Bergström
Sven-Gunnar Bergström
Göran Bergvin
Jesper Berlin
Irja Berntson
Rolf Berntzen
Ztefan Bertha
Gunilla Bertilsson
Jennie Berton

Fredrik Beskow
Millle Bessö
Theres Beswick
Patrick Bethanis
Janna Betzén
Helena Bévengut-Lasson
Catharina Biesèrt
Avdo Bilkanovic
Göran Billeson
Julian Birbrajer
Joakim Birgersson
Marie Birkl
Pia Bise
Ulf Bjelkengren
Kari Bjerke
Ragnhild Bjerkefors
Rich Bjerkeheim
Gustaf L. Bjerne
Catrine Bjulehag
Eva Bjurholm
Hans Bjurling
Max Bjurling
Lars Bjuvenmark
Tomas Bjällerstedt
Christina Björk
Fredrik Björk
Inga Björk
Katarina Björk
Magnus Björk
Mårten Björk
Tove Björk
Bengt Björkbom
Peder Björkegren
Erik Björkgren
Joachim Björklund
Mattias Björklund
Anita Björkman
Fredrik Björkman
Kjell Björkman
Therese Björkman
Ulf Björkman
Bengt Björlin
Larsson Björn
Sonia Björnänge
Axel Björner
Matthias Björner
Marlene Björnfot
Olle Björngreen
Sture Björnson
Henrik Björnsson
Annakarin Björnström
Karin Björnwall
Nicholas Blackmon
Inger Bladh
Stefan Bladh
Daniel van der Blij
Lena Blåsjö
Lena Block
Ingemar Blohm
Elina Blom
Maria Blom
Maude Blomberg
Monica Blomberg
Patrik Blomberg
Roger Blomberg
Kerstin Blomberg Gedda

Malin Blomgren
Anna-Lena Blomquist
Anders Blomqvist
Anna Blomqvist
Gösta Blomqvist
Jan Blomqvist
Karolin L. Blomqvist
Per Blomqvist
Niklas Bodin
Christer Boedeker
Peter Bogren
Gøran Bohlin
Sofia Bohlin
Helen Bohm Andersen
Anna Bokstrom
Aldo Bolle
Anders Boman
Mats Boman
Stefan Boman
Monica Bondesson
Christian Boo
Patrik Book
Calle Borg
Daniel Borg
Glenn Borg
Jonas Borg
Magnus Borg
Stefan Borgius
Kerstin Borgström
Ulf Borin
Hanns Boris
Jonatan Borling
Nina Boström
Torbjörn Boström
Stig Bourwall
Liza Braaw
Clare Bradshaw
Eva Bragesjö
Gerth Bragnå
Cornelia Bramsell
Markus Brandefelt
Andreas Brandell
Björn Brandell
Niklas Brandin
Christian Brandt
Thyra Brandt
Jessica Brannen
Bengt Brantås
Christoffer Bratt
Gustaf Bratt
Kristofer Bratt
Benjamin Braun
Mats Bredberg
Jan-Michael Breider
Marie Bremberg
Charlotte Brems
Jan Brems
Agnete Bretan
Peter Brigge
Jesper Brinck
John Brinck
Rolf van den Brink
Anders Brinnen
Kerstin Brismar
Lennart Broborn
Peter Brockman

Stefan Brockman
Elsa Brodin
Hasse Broms
Eric Brorson
Robin Brorsson
Martin Brorstad
Victoria Broström
Max Brouwers
Zandra Brox
Anne Bruce
Camilla Bruhn
Niklas Brunberg
Staffan Brundell
Lars Brundin
Nikki Brundin
Henrik Brunnsgård
Håkan Brunosson
Hans Brunström
Magnus Brusman
Sara Bruzelius
Marcus Bryngelsson
Lise Bryngemark
Åsvor Brynnel
Urban Brådhe
Theresia Bråkenhielm
Monica Brämstad-Olsson
Emma Bräck
Caroline Bräutigam
Anna von Brömssen
Frans Burghofer
Eleonor Burman
Lars Bygdemark
Jonas Bygdén
Francisco Bueno
Renate Bühler
Jessica Bylund
Rune Bylund
Jenny Byström
Per Byström
Anders Båth
Bosse Bäck
Maria Bäck
Tommy Bäck
Johannes Bäckblom
Uwe Bödewadt
Johan Börjesson
Magnus Börjesson
Sara Cahier
Jeremias Callermo
Pia Callingsjö
Anja Callius
Esther Callmer
Mic Calvert
Denny Calvo
Owe Candow
Sten Canevall
Stig Cannemo
Magnus Carbonnier
Matt Carey
Hasse Carlbaum
Uno Carleke
Emelie Carlén
Johan Carlén
Linda Carlgren
Lisa Carlgren
Thomas Carlgren

Jonas Carlson
Anders Carlsson
Bengt-Göran Carlsson
Björn Carlsson
Bo Carlsson
Borris Carlsson
Göran Carlsson
Helena Carlsson
Ingvar Carlsson
Jan Carlsson
Jan E Carlsson
Jerry Carlsson
Joel Carlsson
Kjell Carlsson
Magnus Carlsson
Malin Carlsson
Mats Carlsson
Miriam Carlsson
Mony Carlsson
Olle Carlsson
Sigfrid Carlsson
Stefan Carlsson
Thomas Carlsson
Tommy Carlsson
Jeanette Carlsson
Karlberg
Maria Carlstedt
Lennart Carlström
Sussie Carlström
Bodil Carlund
Bosse Carsing
Daniel Cavén
Iliana Cavén
Mehri Cavén
Michael Cavén
Ola Cedenheim
Tora Ceder
Peter Cederling
Minna Cederlund
Martin Cejie
Mario Celegin
Magnus Cervin
Pontus Charleville
Aida Chehrehgosha
Camilla Cherry
Michael Child
Alexander Christensen
Mats Christensson
Tomas Christoffersson
Octavian Ciobanu
Charlotta Claesson
Peter Claesson
Staffan Claesson
Sture Claesson
Susanne Claesson
Tony Clementz
Kirk Clendinning
Sarah Cobanoglu
Lotta Collin
Jan Collsiöö
Mary Anne Cornejo
Harriet Corper
Margareta Cortés
Inger J Coster
Alexander Crispin
Marre Crona

Lennart Cronholm
Martin Crook
Måns Cullin
Roger Culmsee
Stefan Dagobert
Annika Dahlberg
Margot Dahlberg
Marianne Dahlberg
Thomas Dahlberg
Bo Dahlgren
Willy Dahlgren
Johan Dahlin
Linda Dahlin
Carina Dahlkvist
Lennart Dahlqvist
Melker Dahlstrand
Rickard Dahlstrand
Jan Dahlström
Jan Håkan Dahlström
Lars Dahlström
David Dahmén
Klas Dalek
Tage Daleljung
Eva Dalin
Perikles Dallas
Inga Damell
Jonas Danielsson
Monica Danielsson
Pelle Danielsson
Peter Danielsson
Sara Danielsson
Sandra Daniloff
Lars Dareberg
Bengt Davidson
Leif Davidsson
Camilla Degerman
Patrick Degerman
Andrina Dehlin
Pernilla Dehlin
Emil Deilert
Jan Delden
Claes Dellwik
Laurent Denimal
Bengt Dernéus
Anders Deros
Clint Dickson
Peter Diedrich
Anna Diehl
Linda Dimeus
Suzana Dimevska
Vildan Dincbas-Renqvist
Jörgen Divert
Senad Dizdar
Gunnar Djerf
Berit Djuse
Bryngel Domeij
Marie-Louise Domeij
Konny Domnauer
Kevin Doyle
Anna Drake-Blomqvist
Alessandra Drakenklo
Per Drejare
Håkan Drugge
Erika Dufmats
Annelie Dufva
Christopher Dunerud

Agnes Duus
Petter Duvander
Christian Düberg
Fredrik Dürichen
Jan Düsing
Miriam Dychawy
Mark Earthy
Ellen Eckemark
Sofia Eckerblad
Joakim Eckerström
Stefan Ed
Anna Edelholm
Lars Edelholm
Bertil Edin
Jan Edlund
Johan Edlund
John Edlund
Jesper Edman
Robert Edman
Vivianne Edorson
Björn Edström
Morgan Edström
Sebastian Edström
Anders Edström Frejman
Monica Edwardsson
Jenny Egeland
Susanne Ehlin
Bruno Ehrs
Paula Eichhorn
Maria Eilertsen
Hannu Einarsson
Hans Eisengarten
Lukas Eisenhauer
Billy Ejdestig
Anders Ek
Bjarne Ek
Daniel Ek
Ulrika Ek
Lars Ekberg
Andreas Ekblad
Lars Ekblad
Malte Ekblom
Bernt Ekdahl
Göran Ekdahl
Håkan Ekebacke
Göran Ekeberg
Mårten Ekehed
Fatima Ekekrantz
Martin Ekelin
Mona Ekelöf
Dag Ekelund
Jenny Ekelund
Gudrun Ekeman-Tolis
Göran Ekeroth
Hans Ekestang
Cecilia Tuss Ekholm
Carlos Eklund
Frida Eklund
Ingegerd Eklund
Jenny Eklund
Martin Eklund
Mats Eklund
Anna-Lena Eklund
 Sterner
Elisabet Ekman
Mats Ekman

Nadja Ekman
Stefan Ekman
Mariana Ekner
Pia Ekstedt-Häggblom
Björn Ekstrand
Helena Ekstrand
Leif Ekstrand
Conny Ekström
Kerstin Ekström
Martina Ekström
Sofia Ekström
Jonas Ekströmer
Jesper Ekvall
Martin Ekwall
Magnus Elander
Jesper Elcar
Christer Elderud
Elin Elderud
Christel Eldrim
Robert Eldrim
Susannah Elers
Olof Elfverson
Anders Eliasson
Carina Eliasson
Charlotte Eliasson
Erica Eliasson
Ingvar Eliasson
Leif Eliasson
Martin Eliasson
Mirjam Eliasson
Ola Eliasson
Owe Ellersten
Holger Ellgaard
Ulrika Ellgaard Hansson
Georg Ellgren
Elliot Elliot
Marta El-Masri
Mohammed El-Masri
Therese Elmgren
Håkan Elmquist
Ola Elmquist
Jonas Elmqvist
Nicklas Elmrin
Lotta Elofsson
Mats Elofsson
Sophie Elsässer
Ruohom Emanuel
Helga Emanuelsson
Jim Emanuelsson
Jonna Emanuelsson
Jon Emsheimer
Andreas Enbuske
Mats Endermark
Patrik Enefjord
David Eng
Maud Eng
Leif Engberg
Ulf Engberg
Leif Engdahl
Lars-Göran E.
 Engelbrektsson
Lisa Engen
Elin Engerström
Erika English
Sara Englund
Tina Englund

Marcos Engman
Per Engman
Christer Engström
Gustav Engström
Hans-Göran Engström
Krister Engström
Lars Engström
Lena Engström
Louise Engström
Marie Engström
Mattias Engström
Pether Engström
Robert Engström
Martina Engvall
Sara Enquist
Anders Enqvist
Kaj Enqvist
Patrik Enström
Claes Enwall
Claude Erbsen
Hans E. Ericson
Inger Ericson
Karin Ericson
Mats Ericson
Pia Ericson
Sabina Ericson
Åke Ericson
Anders Ericsson
Kent H Ericsson
Kerstin Ericsson
Kjell Ericsson
Linnéa Ericsson
Marcus Ericsson
Nils Bertil Ericsson
Peter Ericsson
Roger Ericsson
Sten Ericsson
Ulf Ericsson
Ulrika Ericsson
Henning Eriksen
Ola Erikson
Ammi Eriksson
Anders Eriksson
Anette Eriksson
Ann Eriksson
Anna Eriksson
Annika Eriksson
Beatrice Eriksson
Bjarne Eriksson
Björn Eriksson
Bodil Eriksson
Daniel Eriksson
Emmelie Eriksson
Gunnar Eriksson
Göran Eriksson
Göte Eriksson
Hans Eriksson
Hasse Eriksson
Inge Eriksson
Jennie Eriksson
Joachim Eriksson
Joakim Eriksson
Joel Eriksson
Johan Eriksson
John Eriksson
Jonas Eriksson

Jörgen Eriksson
Karin Eriksson
Kenneth Eriksson
Kjell Eriksson
Kurt Eriksson
Lars Eriksson
Lisa Eriksson
Magnus Eriksson
Malin Eriksson
Maria Eriksson
Mats Eriksson
Micke Eriksson
Mikael Eriksson
Ola Eriksson
Ove Eriksson
Owe Eriksson
Peter Eriksson
Pia Eriksson
Robert Eriksson
Roland Eriksson
Rolf Eriksson
Ronny Eriksson
Stig-Erik Eriksson
Anders Erixon
Josefin Erixon
Arne Erlandsson
Göran Erlandsson
Lisa Erlandsson
Maria Erlandsson
Marie Erlandsson
Raymond Erming
Anna Ernerdahl
Sofia Ernerot
Manilla Ernst
Ingrid Esping
Hans Esselius
Alejandro Estay
Åsa Estvall
Teijo Eteläinen
Eugen
Malin von Euler-Chelpin
Angela Evaldsson
Solbritt Evensson
Jan Everhov
Anna Everitt
Bendie Evertsson
Ulf Fabiansson
Fredrik Fabó
Anna Fagerström
Ola Fagerström
Thomas Fahlander
Bernt-Ola Falck
Christer Falk
Lennart Falk
Lina Falk
Malin Falk
Mikael Falk
Miriam Falk
Susanne Falk
Johan Falkman
Peter Fallberg
Gunnar Fardelin
Alexander Farnsworth
Stefan Fasth
Feri Fazeli
David Feldt

Marc Femenia
David Fennman
Linda Fennman
Lisa Fergusson
Boel Ferm
Arne Fernlund
Gert Fernqvist
Mathias Fernstedt
Bert Fernström
Karina Fernström
Malin Fezehai
Michal Fifowski
José Figueroa
Malin Finborud
Tomas Finger
Ulrika Finnberg
Ulrika Finndahl
Fredrik Fischer
Peter Fischer
Christer Fischier
Sonja Fiskum
Karin Fjell
Leif Fjellström
Dan Fjällman
Helena Flank
Pawel Flato
Jan Fleischmann
Rikard Floridan
Martin Florin
Karl-Erik Flovén
Karin Foberg
Kinga Fogelberg
Lage Fogelberg
Bibbi Fogelqvist
Christer Folkesson
Margareta Folmer
Magnus Fond
Benny Fondén
Elisabet Fornell
Anders Forngren
Patric Fors
Anders Forsberg
Claes Forsberg
Göran Forsberg
Peter Forsberg
Rod Forsberg
Åsa Forsblom
Arne Forsell
Jacob Forsell
Linda Forsell
Nils Forsell
Bengt Forsgren
Karin Forshell
Ida Forslund
Leif Forslund
Johan Forsman
Anders Forsmark
Jan Forsmark
Per-Ola Forss
Harald Fragner
Oskar Franklin
Jonas Fransson
Nils Fransson
Rebecka Fransson
Ulf Fransson
Anders Frantz

Eric Franzén
Gerhard Franzén
Kjell Franzén
Claes Fredelius
Jeanette Fredenberg
Calle Fredin
Ulla Fredin
Magnus Fredlund
Barbro Fredrikson
Erik Fredrikson
Cathrine Fredriksson
Christian Fredriksson
Christina Fredriksson
Håkan Fredriksson
Krister Fredriksson
Lars-Erik Fredriksson
Maria Fredriksson
Örjan Fredriksson
A Camilla Frejman
Gunnar Frennesson
Peter Frennesson
Kåre Frenning
Thomas Freye
Annette Friberg
Dennis Friberg
Hans G Friberg
Johan Frick-Meijer
Lennart Frid
Börje Fridberg
Hans Fridberg
Hasse Fridén
Conny Fridh
Peter Fridlund
Josefin Fridman
Michael Frie
Mikaela Frie
Daniel Fried
Josef Friedinger
Paul Frigyes
Carl-Johan Friman
Sami Friman
Ulrika Frisk
Mikael Fritzing
Jan From
Johan Frost
Karin Fryckstrand
Anders Fryk
Tommy Fryk
Lars-Åke Frykmer
Per Frykner
Börje Frylmark
Caroline Fröberg
Jan Fröberg
Magnus Fröderberg
Erik Fröjdh
Fredrik Funck
Marianne Funck-Olsson
Johan Funke
Christina Furesjö
Ulf Fågelhammar
Andreas Fägerskiöld
Thobias Fäldt
Göran Fält
Kate Gabor
Eivor Gabrielsson
Bengt Gamhov

Enrico Gaoni
Daniel Gardell
Eva Gardholm
Jonas Gardsiö
Lubbe Garell
Lena Garnold
Carola Garpefält
Mats Gauffin
Jenny Gaulitz
Agneta Gavare
Rolf Gavare
Sven Gedda
Thomas Gedminas
Christian Geijer
Claes Gellerbrink
Christian Gennert
Peter Gennert
Bengt af Geijerstam
Peter Gerdehag
Kristofer Gerdt
Peter Gerhard
Wolfgang Gerlach
Emilia Germundsjö
Per Germundsjö
Claus Gertsen
Nashmil Ghassemlou
Dick Gillberg
Linnea Gillberg
Olle Gillberg
Mårten Gjötterberg
Jerry Gladh
Mona och Per Glasare
Fredrik Glawe
Max Goldstein
Conchi Gonzalez
  Lönneryd
Kersti Good
Martin Goodwin
Ciprian Gorga
Per-Åke Gottfridsson
Sebastian Gottfridsson
Vanja Gottlow
Jessica Gow
Uno Gradin
Andreas Grafenauer
Sven Gräfnings
B I Graham
Siv Graham
Daniel Grahn
Jan Grahn
Jörgen Grahn
Roger Granat
Helena Granberg
Klara Granberg
Marcus Granbom
Lena Granefelt
Ingemar Granelli
Laila Granelli
Karin Granholm
Kent Granholm
Bo Granlund
Eddie Granlund
Rolf Granqvist
Karin Granstrand
Walter Grape
Björn Green

Hans Green
Kristina Green
Markus Green
Sahra Green
Stig Green
Horst Grieger
Magnus Grimstedt
Joi Grinde
Marike Grinde
Katarina Grip Höök
Emelie Griplund
Linda Groth
Per Groth
Claes Grundsten
Karin Grute Movin
Inger Gruvsjö
Lennart Grönblad
Johanna Grönlund
Pontus Grönvall
Marie Grönvold
Susann Gson Engqvist
Örs Gubás
Rebecca Gulam
Caroline Gullberg
Anna Gullmark
Oskar Gullmark Jagne
Anna Gummesson
Serkan Gunes
Åke Gunnarson
Stina Gunnarson
Anna Gunnarsson
Joakim Gunnarsson
Lena Gunnarsson
Mats Gunnarsson
Johan Gunséus
Göran Gustafson
Jonas Gustafson
Olle Gustafon
Thomas Gustafson
Torbjörn Gustafson
Anders Gustafsson
Beatrice Gustafsson
Bengt Gustafsson
Emma Gustafsson
Hanna Gustafsson
Henrik Gustafsson
Jan-Peter Gustafsson
Jeppe Gustafsson
Jimmy Gustafsson
Jon Gustafsson
Kjell Gustafsson
Kristina Gustafsson
Kåre Gustafsson
Leif Gustafsson
Magnus Gustafsson
Martin Gustafsson
Mikael Gustafsson
Stefan Gustafsson
Christer Gustavsson
Evelina Gustavsson
Ewa Gustavsson
Ida Gustavsson
Jan Gustavsson
Jens Gustavsson
Kent-Åke Gustavsson
Malin Gustavsson

Niklas Gustavsson
Staffan Gustavsson
Veronica Gustavsson
Maria Gutebring
Susanne Gyllenlöf
Folke Günther
Aina Gürlet
Björn Gävert
Anna-Karin Göransson
Christer Göransson
Gunilla Göransson
Niklas Göransson
Pier Göransson
Sara Göransson
Anders Görlinge
Ulrika Göthenqvist
Ragnhild Haarstad
Lars Hadders
Bertil Hagberg
Charlotta Hagberg
Niklas Hagberg
Sven-Gillis Hagberg
Tomas Hagberg
Jimmie Hagblad
Stina Hagdahl
Stefan Hagel
Emil Hagelin
Micke Hager
Gudrun Hagerö
John Hagestål
Anders Haglund
Anki Haglund
Bosse Haglund
Monica Haglund
Ove Haglund
Tore Hagman
Jan Hagström
Anita Hakala
Fia Halén
Clara Hall
Ulrika Hall
Diana Hallberg
Lars Hallberg
Lars-Olof Hallberg
Peter Hallberg
Maya Halldén
Gustaf Halldin
Dennis Hallgren
Mats Hallgren
Ronald Hallgren
Barbro Hallin
Göran Hallin
Susanne Hallmann
Matilda Hallnor
Linus Hallsenius
Björn Hallström
Lilian Hallström
Patrick Hallström
Ingemar Hällström
Krister Halvars
Lasse Halvarsson
Torleif Halvorsen
Inger Hamark
Peter Hamberg
Joachim Hamilton
Bibi Hammar

Christopher
  Hammarborg
Bo Hammarlund
Hans Hammarskiöld
Agneta Hammarstedt
Mats Hammarstedt
Stig Hammarstedt
Rosita Hammarsten
Niclas Hammarström
Per Hammenvik
Nazira Hammoud
Susanne Hamne
Bertil Hanås
Malcolm Hanes
Mark Hanlon
Johanna Hanno
Jimmy Hansen
Paul Hansen
Pia Hansen
Johan Hansén
Anders Hansson
Dan Hansson
Emma Hansson
Georg Hansson
Gunte Hansson
Hans-Göran Hansson
Henrik Hansson
Jon Hansson
Karin Hansson
Krister Hansson
Leif Hansson
Maria Hansson
Martin Hansson
Mikael Hansson
Nicolas Hansson
Pierre Hansson
Sofia Hansson
Stefan Hansson
Ulf Hansson
Per Hanstorp
Susanna Haraldsson
Staffan Hardie
Catarina Harling
Angelica Harms
Anna Harrysson
Sune Harrysson
Anne Hartikainen
Henrik Hartman
Magnus Hartman
Seif al Hasani
Lina Haskel
Lisa Hasselgren
Therese Hasselryd
Joachim Haux
Bertil Havdelin
Sasha Hebib
Göran Heckler
Frida Hedberg
Johan Hedenberg
Louise Hederstierna
Per-Åke Hedin
Anders Hedlund
Annelie Hedlund
Jane Hedlund
Kristofer Hedlund
Olof Hedlund

Ulf Hedlund
Bo Hedman
Per-Henrik Hedman
Stig OE Hedman
Ingrid Hedström
Jenny Hedström
Åke Hedström
Jim Heikkinen
Lena Heiman
Jenny Hein
Clas Heinebäck
Melker Heintz
Cecilia Heisser
Sonja Hejdeman
Thomas Hejdenbäck
Lasse Hejdenberg
Aron Hejdström
Tarja Hekkala
Pär Helander
Adam Helbaoui
Mia Helgelin
Anders Helgesson
Bruno Helgesson
Torbjörn Helgesson
Anna Hellberg
Daniel Hellberg
Jörgen Hellberg
Malin Hellberg
Michael Helldén
Peter Hellén
Anders Hellgren
Cathrine Hellman
Erik Hellquist
Eva Hellquist
Jörgen Hellquist
Eva Hellsten
Hanna Hellsten
Mikael Hellsten
Simon Hellsten
Anders Hellstrand
Annika Hellström
Stefan Hellström
Tomas Hellström
Cecilia Helsing
Sophie Helsing
Andreas Hemb
Margareta Hemberg
Johnny Henestål
Rickard Henley
Jonna Hennig
Fredrik Henning
Marcus Henningsson
Mats Henningsson
Sten-Åke Henningsson
Carl Hennix
Niklas Henrikczon
Ellika Henrikson
Andreas Henriksson
Carola Henriksson
Eva Henriksson
Helena Henriksson
Kenneth Henriksson
Tina Henriksson
Camilla Henrysson
David Herdies
Hans Hermansson

Per Arne Hermansson
Svante Hermansson
Lena Herrmann
Mats Herrström
Jon Hertov
Katarina Hertzman-
  Ericson
Lo Hertzman-Ericson
Fanny Hesslegård
Maria Hessleryd
Niklas Heurgren
Jörgen Hildebrandt
Andreas Hillergren
Linda Himsel
Roy Himsel
Calle Hinderson
Jan Hinderson
Ann Hingström
Anita Hjalmarsson
Mats Hjalmarsson
Raija Hjalmarsson
Simon Hjalmarsson
Anna Hjertstrand
Håkan Hjortek
Lena Hjälmgren
Kerstin Hjärpe
Sasha Hodzic
Peter Hoelstad
C-O Hofberg
Maria Hoff Rudhult
Martin Hoffborn
Caroline Hoffman
Ulrika Hoffman
Göran Hofstedt
Mikael Hofverberg
Ewa Holdar
Magnus Holgersson
Mattias Holgersson
Nils-Olof Holgersson
Daniel Holking
Tommy Holl
Niklas Holm
Susanne Holm
Håkan Holmbeck
Barbro Holmberg
Conny Holmberg
Fredrik Holmberg
Hasse Holmberg
Kent Holmberg
Linda Holmberg
Martina Holmberg
Olle Holmberg
Ulf Holmberg
Maud Holmberg Klyft
Margit Holmén
Pär Holmén
Mats Holmertz
Bengt Holmgren
Bjarne Holmgren
Karin Holmgren
Lars Holmgren
Paulina Holmgren
Annagreta Holmquist
Bjarne Holmquist
Lars Holmquist
Mats Holmquist

247

Annarika Holmqvist
David Holmqvist
Tobias Holmqvist
Erik Holmstedt
Ulf H Holmstedt
Ann-Christin Holmström
Inger Holmström
Janne Holst
Axel Holtin
Larry Holward
Anders Honkamaa
Mats Honkamaa
Joanna Honkanen
Pieter ten Hoopen
Kristin Horn
Jörgen Hornsten-Gran
Peter Horvath
Solveig Hovold
Bertil Howegård
Lynne Howell Wiklander
Teres Huitema
Jim Hujanen
Patrick Hult
Christer Hultberg
Martin Hultén
Fredrik Hultin
Tanya Hultman
Håkan Humla
Maths Husander
Klara Hussénius
Björn Huzell
Mårten Huzell
Tommy Hvitfeldt
Arne Hyckenberg
Lennart Hyse
Isobel Håkanlind
Sören Håkanlind
Mats Håkanson
Albert Håkansson
Ann-Sofie Håkansson
Bonny Håkansson
David Håkansson
Håkan Håkansson
Isabel Håkansson
Jenny Håkansson
Lars Håkansson
Peter Håkansson
Josefin Hållbus
Sara Hårdén
Folke Hårrskog
Lars Hägg
Jonas Hägglund
Krister Hägglund
Lars Hägglund
Rory Hägglund
Ruaridh Hägglund
Robin Häggqvist
Marcus Häggström
Krister Hällgren
Roger Hällhag
Anna Hämäläinen
Fredrik Härenstam
Helga Härenstam
Johan Högberg
Robert Högfeldt
Christer Höglund

Gösta Höglund
Jessica Höglund
Stefan Höglund
Christian Högstedt
Åsa Höjer
Karoline Höög
Marco Iaconelli
Malin Idén
Roger Iderman
Johan Idstam
Adam Ihse
Lars Ingels
Rolf Ingemansson
Nichlas Ingemarsson
Gunilla Inger
Fanny Irving
Johan Isacson
Ulf Isacson
Johan Isacsson
Ariann Isaksson
Jimmy Isaksson
Martin Isaksson
Per-Erik Isaksson
Robin Isaksson
Sofie Isaksson
Annika Ivarsson
Christina Ivarsson
Håkan Ivarsson
Martina Iverus
Mauricio Izquierdo
Arendi Jaak
Kevin Jacob
Irene Jacobson
Jacob Jacobson
Karl Jacobson
Leif Jacobsson
Petra Jacobsson
Stellan Jacobsson
Bente Jakobsen
Krister Jakobsson
Maja Jakobsson
Mikael Jakobsson
Patric Jakobsson
Pär Erik Jakobsson
Torbjörn Jakobsson
Traudi Jakobsson
Richard Jalakas
Maria Janås
Ola Janhall
Gregor Janhed
Petra Jankov
Anna Jansson
Ann-Sofie Jansson
Claes Jansson
Jenny Jansson
Jesper Jansson
Jessica Jansson
Johannes Jansson
Karin Jansson
Lars Jansson
Linda Jansson
Maria Jansson
Mats B Jansson
Mattias Jansson
Mikael Jansson
Peter Jansson

Sofie Jansson
Stefan Jansson
Tobias Jansson
Ulf Jansson
Anna M Jarås
Andreas Jarblad
Daniel Jarblad
Karin Jardbrant
Per Jardemyr
Bengt Jardstam
Sara Jardstam
Kim Jarl
Lars-Gunnar Jarl
Marcus Jarl
Per Jarl
Tommy Jarnbrink
Fredrik Jarnhag
Johan Javinder
Christer Jegbert
Finn Jensen
Rune Jensen
Johan Jeppsson
Anders Jernbom
Daniel Jernström
Stefan Jerrevång
Björn Jersby
Johan Jersby
Satish Jeswani
Peter Jigerström
Harriet Jildergård
Malin Jilkén
Irina Jillker
Lars-Einar Jillker
Jan Johannessen
Per Johannessen
Ingmar Johanson
P.Roland Johanson
Tomas Johanson
Anders Johansson
Angelica Johansson
Anita Johansson
Anna Johansson
Anna-Karin Johansson
Anna-Lena Johansson
Annika Johansson
Arne Johansson
Bass Johansson
Bernt E Johansson
Birgit Johansson
Bo Johansson
Bosse Johansson
Britta Johansson
Britt-Mari Johansson
Bror Johansson
Calle Johansson
Camilla Johansson
Carl Magnus Johansson
Christina Johansson
Daniel Johansson
Elin Johansson
Erik Johansson
Fredrik Johansson
Gerhard Johansson
Gunnar Johansson
Gunnel Johansson
Göran Johansson

Göran G. Johansson
Helen Johansson
Helena Johansson
Henrik Johansson
Håkan Johansson
Ida Johansson
Ingegerd Johansson
Ivar Johansson
Jan Johansson
Jenny Johansson
Jessika Johansson
Joakim Johansson
Johanna Johansson
Jörgen Johansson
Kjell Johansson
Lars Johansson
Lars-Gunnar Johansson
Lena Johansson
Lennart Johansson
Magnus Johansson
Marcus Johansson
Margareta Johansson
Maria Johansson
Marie Johansson
Martin Johansson
Mattias Johansson
Mikael Johansson
Monica Johansson
Naomi Johansson
Nicke Johansson
Nils Olof Johansson
Patrik Johansson
Per Johansson
Peter Johansson
Petter Johansson
Sara Johansson
Simon Johansson
Sofia Johansson
Sophia Johansson
Staffan Johansson
Stefan Johansson
Stig-Arne Johansson
Thomas Johansson
Thommy Johansson
Tomas Johansson
Ulf Johansson
Ulrika Johansson
Vicky Johansson
Bertil K Johansson-Bräck
Lennart Johanzon
Sören Johnson
Annika Johnsson
Patrik Johnsson
Thomas Johnsson
Mark Joiner
Leif Joley
Andreas Jonasson
Eva Jonasson
Mikael Jonasson
Jonas Jonerup
Per Jonhed
Lizette Jonjic
Fredrik Jonson
Anders Jonsson
Annette Jonsson
Annika Jonsson

Carl-Axel Jonsson
Christer Jonsson
Claes Jonsson
Erik Jonsson
Helga Jonsson
Lars Jonsson
Lina Jonsson
Maria Jonsson
Marita Jonsson
Mattias Jonsson
Ove Jonsson
Petra Jonsson
Ulf B. Jonsson
Zarah Jonsson
Agne Josefsson
Caroline Josefsson
Bill Jubner
Lars Juhlin
Bengt Jungberg
Stig Jungberg
Håkan Junkes
Kristina Junzell
Janos Jurka
Reimar Torkil Juul
Ernst Jünger
Maria Jynnskog
Leif Jäderberg
Christer Järeslätt
Anders Järkendal
Jonas Järmén
Linda Jönér
Annica Jönsson
Björn Jönsson
Bo Ingvar Jönsson
Lena Jönsson
Lennart Jönsson
Martin Jönsson
Mattias Jönsson
Ola Jönsson
Peter Jönsson
Rolf Jönsson
Stig-Åke Jönsson
Sven Jönsson
Tomaz Jönsson
Urban Jörén
Andreas Jörgensen
Jacob Jörgensen
Lotta Jörgensen
Per-Anders Jörgensen
Eric Jöråker
Nina Kaikkonen
Andreas Kalliaridis
Béatrice Karjalainen
Emma Karlberg
Moa Karlberg
Annika Karlbom
Peter Karlbrink
Göran Karlgren
Mikael Karlin
Magnus Karlson
Sören Karlson
Ami Karlsson
Anders Karlsson
Anna Karlsson
Benny Karlsson
Birgitta Karlsson

Daniel Karlsson
Erik Karlsson
Gerd Karlsson
Gun Karlsson
Gunilla Karlsson
Gustaf Karlsson
Gustav Karlsson
Hans Karlsson
Jan Erik Karlsson
Jens Karlsson
Johnny Karlsson-Kern
Kenneth Karlsson
Kent Karlsson
Kjell Karlsson
Lars Karlsson
Lennart Karlsson
Lili-Ann Karlsson
Lina Karlsson
Mats Karlsson
Mikael Karlsson
Moa Karlsson
Morgan Karlsson
Nicklas Karlsson
Nils-Åke Karlsson
Pontus Karlsson
Ralf Karlsson
Therése Karlsson
Tomas Karlsson
Torbjörn Karlsson
Viveca Karlsson
Åke Karlsson
Anders Karlstam
Eva-Carin Karlströms Kling
Mia Karlsvärd
Tommy Karonen
Magnus Karperyd
Pernilla Karström
Stergios Kastoris
Kaisa Kaulanen
Jorma Kaunonen
Johan Kaving
Nicolaus Kedegren
Anna Kejler
Martin Kemani
Kristina Keyzer Hallman
Sayed Khatib
Rickard Kilström
Andreas Kindler
Göran Kindwall
Diana Kirjonen
Caroline Kirkhouse
Jan Kivisaar
Anna Zoila Kjellander
John Kjellberg
Peter Kjellerås
Malou Kjellsson
Jan Kjerrud
Frida Klang
Vojta Klecka
Christian Kleinhenz
Thomas Klenze
Anders Kling
S Åke Klinga
David Klingvall
Fredrik Klingwall

Jenny Klingwall
Anna Klinkert
Anna Klint
Anna Klintasp
Chris Klug
Mattias Klum
Miriam Klyvare
Calle Klövstad
Magda Kniola
Peter Knopp
Johan Knutsson
Per Knutsson
Matilda Kock
Kari Kohvakka
Rolf Kokkonen
Malin Koldenius
Hans Kongbäck
Mikael Konttinen
Jaan Koort
Helena Korhonen
Mika Korhonen
Pekka Koskenvoima
Pavel Koubek
Petter Koubek
Lars Krabbe
Gabriella Kræpelien
Martina Kramsova
Julie Krause
Kristian Krebs
Arne Krenzisky
My Kreuger
Tobias Kreuter
Ingela Krieger
Georg Kristiansen
Janina Kristiansen
Per Kristiansen
Bo-Göran Kristofferson
Karl-Gustaf Kristoffersson
Martin von Krogh
Pelle Kronestedt
Susanne Kronholm
Martin Krook
Linda Kroon
Maria Kroon
Peter Kroon
Nic Kruys
Dan Kullberg
Elin Kullerstrand
Linda Kumblad
Jennie Kumlin
Michelle Kuronen
Jan Kwarnmark
Elisa Kvennborn
Göran Kvick
Susanna Kvist
Gunnar Jerry Kålbäck
Peter Kåretun
Anders Kårlid
Marcus Källander
Lena Källberg
Anders Källen
Mats Källstig
Kim Källström
Marie-Louise Källström
Niklas Kämpargård

Anders Kämpe
Henrik Känngård
Darlene Kärnström
Kate Kärrberg
Stina Kätting
Lars Köhler
Olga Köhn
Tomas Königsson
Mikael Laaksonen
Conny Lagé
Jocke Lagercrantz
Lars Lagerqvist
Lotta Lagerson
Eva-Lisa Lagerström
Torbjörn Laggar
Niklas Lagström
Ulrika Lahti
Enno Laidla
Karin Laine
Katrin Laine
Liisa Laine
Sakari Laine
Bo Lambert
Staffan Lamm
Christer Lampa
Bengt Landahl
Mathias Landefjord
Linda Landenberg
Mats Landin
Jennie Landstedt
Katarina Landström
Lena Landvall
Kjell Landås
Johan Lange
Mårten Lange
Iwan Langermo
Carlo Langfos
Måns Langhjelm
Lennart Lannfjäll
Lisa Lannfjäll
Inga Lantz
Inger Lantz
Adam Larsson
Anna Larsson
Cecilia Larsson
Christina Larsson
Christine Larsson
Daniel Larsson
Emma Larsson
Erik Larsson
Fredrik Larsson
Gabriella Larsson
Helena Larsson
Ingvar Larsson
Jeanette Larsson
Jenny Larsson
Jens Larsson
Kalle Larsson
Katarina Larsson
Kenneth Larsson
Kent Larsson
Krister Larsson
Kristian Larsson
Lars Larsson
Leif Larsson
Liselotte Larsson

Maud Larsson
Niklas Larsson
Per Larsson
Peter Larsson
Rickard Larsson
Robert Larsson
Roger Larsson
Rolf Larsson
Royne Larsson
Rune Larsson
Sara Larsson
Stefan Larsson
Tom Larsson
Tommy Larsson
Torbjörn Larsson
Tord Larsson
Uno Larsson
Björn Larsson Ask
Erika Laur Rosenbäck
Ahti Laurila
Christian Laurila
Liselotte Laurila
Pernilla Lavesson
Miko Lazic
Anders Leander
Andreas Lebzien
Albert Lechleitner
Rustan Lefin
Stefan Lehtilä
Erland Leide
Mikael Leijon
Nina Leijonhufvud
Izabelle Leijström
Per Leijström
Maud Leindahl
Pontus Leitzler
Morgan Lejon
Ann-Christine Lekberg
Anders Lekholm
Monica Leksell
Jonas Lemberg
Erja Lempinen
David Lenander
Maria Lendi-Holmberg
Frida Lenholm
Magnus Lennartsson
Christian Leo
Erik Leonsson
Erik Leppälä
Elise Leppänen
Fredrik Lewander
Malin Leveau
Johan Lewenhaupt
Nils-Göran Levin
Annika Lewinson
Morgan
Jakob Leykauff
Jenny Leyman
Laura Leyshon-Thuresson
Leif Liard
Michael Lichtenstein
Kristin Lidell
Michael Liden
Carina Lidfeldt
Åke Lidzell
Jan Liedholm

Siri Liedholm
Julia Lilenthal Khelef
Lars Lilieqvist
Andreas Lilja
Jessika Lilja
Peter Lilja
Lars Liljendahl
Helena Liljestrand
Kalle Lind
Marion Lind
Paulina Lind
Rolf Lind
Andreas Lindahl
Katarina Lindahl
Tina Lindahl
Björn Lindberg
Calinge Lindberg
Christofer Lindberg
Dan Lindberg
Daniel Lindberg
Henrik Lindberg
Pia Lindberg
Sofie Lindberg
Stefan Lindberg
Christopher Lindbergh
Marcus Lindblad
Johan Lindblom
Tommy Lindblom
Gunnar Linde
Martin Lindeborg
Emma Lindell
Frank Lindell
Petra Lindell
Elisabet Linden
Anders Lindén
Frida Lindén
Hans Lindén
Larseric Lindén
Lisa Lindén
Mikael Lindén
Ann Linder
Alf Linderheim
Anders Lindgren
Björn Lindgren
Carin Lindgren
Håkan Lindgren
Jonas Lindgren
Kåge Lindgren
Peter Lindgren
Thor Lindgren
Anders Lindh
Camilla Lindh
Carina Lindh
Marcus Lindh
Owe Lindh
Sam Lindh
Jenny Lindhe
Elias Lindhoff
Anders Lindholm
Christian Lindholm
David Lindholm
Lisa Lindholm
Susanne Lindholm
Jan-Erik Lindkvist
Tove Lindkvist
Roger Lindman

Jan Lindmark
Lars Lindner
Charlotta Lindow
Mathias Lindow
Jonas Lindquist
Anna Lindqvist
Louise Lindqvist
Sanna Lindqvist
Therese Lindqvist
Anna-Maria Lindqvist
Arrue
Kurt Lindroth
Per Lindroth
Hans-Ebbe Lindskog
Björn Lindström
Daniel Lindström
Dick Lindström
Jeanette Lindström
Joachim Lindström
Kent Lindström
Linda Lindström
Max Lindström
Per Lindström
Sebastian Lindström
Fredrik Lindvall
Johan Lindvall
Jan Linered
Richard Lineruth
Eva Linnér
Albin Linnstrand
Jann Lipka
Magda Lipka Falck
Lena Lipschütz
Lotta Lisslö
Anna Littorin
Kerstin Ljung
Leif Ljung
Magnus Ljung
Petter Ljungberg
Anna Ljungbäck
Marianne Ljunggren
Sven Ljunggren
Johan Ljungström
Maria Ljungström
Jan Ljungwaldh
Malin Loiske Svanberg
Michael Lokner
Mona Loose
Tobias Loré
Denny Lorentzen
Mikael Lorin
Merja Louka
Daniel Lovborn
Martin Lumsby
Annika Lund
Jonas Lund
Öyvind Lund
Johan Lundahl
Pontus Lundahl
Fredrik Lundbeck
Berit Lundberg
Daniel Lundberg
Fredrik Lundberg
Hans Lundberg
Jan Lundberg
Jenny Lundberg

Patrik Lundberg
Petra Lundberg
Anders Lundblad
Mattias Lundblad
Jonas Lundbladh
Beatrice Lundborg
Catrin Lundeberg
Mattias Lundell
Stefan Lundell
Christian Lundgren
Fredrik Lundgren
Jan Lundgren
Kicki Lundgren
Lasse Lundgren
Mikael Lundgren
Owe Lundgren
Daniel Lundh
Eva Lundh
Andreas Lundholm
Henry Lundholm
Rebecca Lundholm
Anders Lundin
Jan Lundin
Jenny Lundin
Per-Axel Lundin
Veronika Lundin
Anders Lundkvist
Lennart Lundkvist
Carola Lundmark
Susanna Lundquist
Anna-Lena Lundqvist
Elisabeth Lundqvist
Petra Lundqvist
Anders Lundström
Camilla Lundström
Fredrik Lundström
Mikael Lundström
Sonja Lundström
Jonas Lundvall
Peter Lydén
Per Långström
Jonas Lägerud
Bengt Olof Löf
Claes Löfgren
Henrik Löfgren
Kai Löfgren
Dan Löfquist
Karl-Einar Löfqvist
Thomas Löfqvist
Sören Löfvenhaft
Anders Lönn
Sophie Lönn
Magnus Lönnegren
Jahn Lönneryd
Anders Lönning
Roger Lönnqvist
Thomas Lönnström
Ann-Margreth Löthman
Inger Löv
Sophia Lövgren
Vanja Lövgren
Mikael Löwgren
Jesper Lövkvist
Malin Lövqvist
Sara Mac Key
Peter MacCormack

Liz Madebrink
Eduardo Madriaga
Adam Madsen
Per Magnuson
Arne Magnusson
Catarina Magnusson
Cim Magnusson
Jens Magnusson
Jonas Magnusson
Peter Magnusson
Roine Magnusson
Anne Majakari
Ramon Maldonado
Anders Malm
Hans Malm
Kahrin Malm
Margaretha Malm
Ulrika Malm
Åsa Malm
Anders Malmberg
Arne Malmberg
Leif Malmberg
Emil Malmborg
Fredrik Malmborg
Karin Malmhav
John Malmlund
Anna Malmqvist
Lars Malmqvist
Sara Malmqvist
Lars Malmros
Ewa Malmsten
Jesper Malmsten
Martin Malmsten
Hans Malmström
Johan Malmström
Chris Maluszynski
Hans Malv
Herbert Marcher
Joakim Marcko
Max Marcus
Mark Markefelt
Johan Markusson
Paul Marshall
Niklas Martinson
Olle Martinson
Magnus Martinsson
Finn Martner
André Maslennikov
Giorgio Masnikosa
Gunnar Mathiason
Anne-Marie Mattiasson
Anders Mattsson
Aron Mattsson
Erik Mattsson
Jan Mattsson
Katarina Mattsson
Margaretha Mattsson
Stefan Mattsson
Anders Mattsson-Tholén
Niklas Maupoix
Eva Mautino
Stephan Maxkellen
Jorgos Mazarakis
Linda Mazzi
Anna McGovern
Klas Mede

Petra Mede
Eva Medin Johansson
Bernhard Meijer
Hans Meijner
Ellinor Melander
Johan Melander
Karl Melander
Christian Melin
Stefan Melin
Daniel Melinder
Fredrik Mellert
Alexej Melnikov
Paul Merkland
Peter Mesch
Kim Metso
Charles Metzmaa
Mariina Metzmaa
Mikael Metzmaa
Amadeus Meyer
Linus Meyer
Lars Michelgård
Laila Mikalsen
Linda Mikkonen
Jack Mikrut
Alex Mitchell
Dragan Mitrovic
Anna Moberg
Bengt Jörgen Moberg
Helena Moberg
Irene Moberg
Elin Mockelind
Jonas Modig
Niklas Modig
Lasse Modin
Mehrdad Modiri
Håkan Mohlin
David Molarin
Hjalmar Molin
Petra Molin
Erika Moll
Börje Monsen
Ulla Montan
Henrik Montgomery
Felipe Morales Letelier
Christina Morberg
Daniel Mott
Laura Mpagi
Riccardo Mugnosso
Mette Muhli
Janne Muhonen
Mikael Muhr
Goran Mulahusic
Miguel Muñoz Rubilar
Timo Murberger
Josip Mustapic
Brita-Johanna Mutka
Dietrich Müller
Peter Mångs
Annelie Månsson
Erik Månsson
Jens Månsson
Lennart Månsson
Susanne Måringer
Tora Mårtens
Erik Mårtensson
Gustav Mårtensson

Sofia Mårtensson
Mitra Mäki
Perra Mäki
Katriina Mäkinen
Ragnhild Möller
Björn Möllerström
Kristian Möllesjö
Olle Mörlund
Leena Möttus
Noel Naanep
Mohammad Hassan
Nadjafi
Hillevi Nagel
Juki Nakamura
Anette Nantell
Kim Naylor
Carl-Olov Neider
John Nelander
Niklas Nelldal
Barbro Nelly
Rikhard Nelson
Susanna Németh
Peter Nerström
Isabelle Nesterud
Eva Neveling
Maria Niemi
Veronika Niemi
Petra Nieto
Jenny Niia
Greger Ulf Nilson
Mats Nilson
Agneta Nilsson
Alexander Nilsson
Anders Nilsson
Andreas Nilsson
Anna Nilsson
Ann-Kristin Nilsson
Björn Nilsson
Bosse Nilsson
Bo-Åke Nilsson
Cecilia Nilsson
Dan Nilsson
Daniel Nilsson
David Nilsson
Dick Nilsson
Fredrik Nilsson
Frida Nilsson
Gunnar Nilsson
Gustaf Nilsson
Henrik Nilsson
Inge Nilsson
Ingemar Nilsson
Ingrid Nilsson
Ingvar Nilsson
Jenny Nilsson
Jessica Nilsson
Johan Nilsson
Johanna Nilsson
Josefine Nilsson
Julian Nilsson
Karolina Nilsson
Katerina Nilsson
Kent Nilsson
Kicki Nilsson
Kjell Nilsson
Lars Nilsson

Lars-Olof Nilsson
Lennart Nilsson
Linus Nilsson
Magnus Nilsson
Malin Nilsson
Maria Nilsson
Martina Nilsson
Mattias Nilsson
Max Nilsson
Monika Nilsson
Nils Nilsson
Nils-Börje Nilsson
Nils-Erik Nilsson
Noomi Nilsson
Olle Nilsson
Per Nilsson
Peter Nilsson
Petter Nilsson
Robert Nilsson
Rune Nilsson
Stefan Nilsson
Stellan Nilsson
Stig-Göran Nilsson
Stina Nilsson
Sun Nilsson
Therese Nilsson
Thomas Nilsson
Tomas Nilsson
Tony Nilsson
Ulf Nilsson
Ulrica Nilsson
Åsa Nilsson
Daniel Nilsson Ranta
Thomas Christopher
Nilzhon
Katarina Nimmervoll
Peter Nobis
Sten Nolin
Clara Norbeck
Erik Norberg
Lars Norberg
Kent Nordbakk
Peter Nordbakk
Christel Nordberg
Marie Nordberg
Sofia Nordberg
Truls Nordberg
Sten-Olof Nordblom
Bengt Nordborg
Jan Nordén
Magnus Norden
Teresia Nordenborg
Sara Nordenhäll
Cecilia Nordenstam
Ulla Nordfors
Caroline Nordgren
Helene Nordgren
Lisa Nordgren
Mattias Nordgren
Brita Nordholm
Björn Nordien
Kajsa Nordin
Lars Nordin
Per-Olof Nordin
Pär-Erik Nordin
Caroline Nordlund

Håkan Nordlöf
Jenny Nordquist
Fredrik Nordqvist
Cecilia Nordstrand Alin
Henrik Nordström
Håkan Nordström
Jan Nordström
Jens Nordström
Natascha Nordström
Nicklas Nordström
Sivert Nordström
Stefan Nordström
Johanna Norén
Niklas Norén
Nils-Johan Norenlind
Johan Norin
Lars-Göran Norlin
Stig Norling
Birgitta Norman
Elin Norman
Morgan Norman
Åsa Norman
Matilda Norrman
Anders Norrsell
Efwa Norrvi
Ulf Norström
Håkan Nunstedt
Cletus Nelson Nwadike
Elsa Nyberg
Kenneth Nyberg
Pär Nyberg
Ragnar Nyberg
Fredrik Nyblad
Helena Nyblom
Peter Nyblom
Per-Erik Nybäck
Lars-Åke Nygren
Miriam Nygren
Nils-Erik Nygren
Staffan Nygren
Tomas Nygren
Tommy Nygren
Bjarne Nygård
Rickard Nygårds
Ralph Nykvist
Henrik Nylander
Torbjörn Nylén
Gunn Nylend
Niklas Nylin
Carolina Nylund
Erik Nylund
Sarah Nylund
Fredrik Nyman
Jonas Nyman
Lars Nyman
Martina Nyman
Mats Nymberg
Lars Nyqvist
Bo Nystrand
Ann H Nyström
Anna Nyström
Annsofie Nyström
Hans Nyström
Irène Nyström
Johanna Nyström
Marie Nyström

Stig Nyström
Sven Nyström
Helena Närä
Erik Näslund
Ingvar Näslund
Lars Näslund
Olof Näslund
Mattias Nääs
Karin Beate Nøsterud
Josefina Oddsberg
Göran Odefalk
Lovisa Odelstierna
Johan Oden
Anna-Maria Odén
Göran Odén
Lasse Odin
Cecilia Odlind
Sven Odqvist
Valentin Ogneov
Camilla O'Gorman
Jan Ohlin
Tobias Ohls
Ann-Sofi Ohlson
Oskar Ohlson
Claes Ohlsson
Jens Ohlsson
Perry Ohlsson
Peter Ohlsson
Johan Okker
Johanna Olander
Catarina Olausson
Ingemar Olausson
Jan Olby
William Olebring
Lars Olefeldt
Rikke Grangaard Olesen
Annalena Olofsdotter
Göran Olofsson
Joel Olofsson
Karl-Uno Olofsson
Marita Olofsson
Michael Olofsson
Peter Olofsson
Torbjörn Olofsson
Veronica Olofsson
Ann Olsén
Hans Olsen
Malin Olsén
Rikard Olsen
Tage Olsin
Björn Olson
Kenneth Olson
Olavi Olson
Anders Olsson
Andreas Olsson
Anna Olsson
Anne-Mari Olsson
Bo-Lennart Olsson
Bosse Olsson
Brita Olsson
Britt-Mari Olsson
Christine Olsson
Elle Olsson
Erik Olsson
Eva-Lena Olsson
Fredrik Olsson

Frida Olsson
Gunilla Olsson
Göran Olsson
Ida Olsson
Ingemar Olsson
Karl-Erik Olsson
Leif Olsson
Lena Olsson
Linda Olsson
Mats Olsson
Mattias Olsson
Roger Olsson
Rolf Olsson
Stina Olsson
Tim Olsson
Tomas Olsson
Tord Olsson
Ulrika Olsson
Magnus Olstenius
Elisabet Omsén
Marie Orbilt
Rikard Orell
Fernando Orellana
Maria Orre
Johannes Ortner
Anders Oscarsson
Johan Oscarsson
Peter Oscarsson
Fredrik Oskarson
Anna Ossung
Mats Ossung
Tomasz Oszmian
Susanne Otterberg
Björn Otterdahl
Anna Ottosson
Christina Ottosson
Lasse Ottosson
Tobias Ottosson
Staffan Ovesson
Malin Pahlm
Noémi Pál
Karin Pallbo
Charlotta Palm
Johan Palm
Kristina Palm
Lars Palm
Mia Palm
Patrik Palm
Sonja Palm
Frida Palmbo
Marcus Palmgren
Markus Palmving
Björn Palovaara
Victoria Pamlényi
Jesper Panser
Julia Paraskova
Lars Parbring
Stefan Parmark
John Parnefjord
Carolina Pascual
Söderbaum
Jennie Passvik
Christopher Patience
Stefan Patkos
Jonas Paulsson
Kenneth Paulsson

Viktor Paulsson
Anne Pavoson
Daniel Pedersen
Kristian Pedersen
Lasse Pedersen
Helena Pehrson
Lars Pehrson
Nestor Peixoto Noya
Louise Pekkanen
Jörgen Penn
Ralf Pergande
Alf Pergeman
Boppe Perhamn
Hampus Perhamn
Annika Perhans
Solveig Perklen
Magnus Perlow
Anders Persson
Andreas Persson
Arne Persson
Bert Persson
Björn Persson
Britta-Stina Persson
Christer Persson
Elisabet Persson
Eric Persson
Fredrik Persson
Gunnar Persson
Göran Persson
Holger Persson
Jan-Olle Persson
Johan Persson
Johannes Persson
Jonas Persson
Julia Persson
Jörgen Persson
Kaj Persson
Kjell-Åke Persson
Leif Persson
Magnus Persson
Maria Persson
Marie Persson
Martin Persson
Mats Persson
Mikael Persson
Olle Persson
Patric Persson
Rigmor Persson
Staffan Persson
Stefan Persson
Sven Persson
Thea Persson
Thomas Persson
Thorsten Persson
Tobias Persson
Tony Persson
Tove Persson
Ulf Persson
Mikael Pertmann
Jonas Peterson
Anders Petersson
Dan Petersson
Gun Petersson
Henrik Petersson
Håkan Petersson
Jesper Petersson

Linda Petersson
Marie Petersson
Rolf Petersson
Susanne Petersson
Jonas Peterström
Ivo Petko
Andreas Pettersson
Bengt Pettersson
Benny Pettersson
Christer Pettersson
Dan Pettersson
Emma Pettersson
Erik Pettersson
Eva-Lotta Pettersson
Fredrik Pettersson
Jessica Pettersson
Johan Pettersson
Kjell Pettersson
Liv Pettersson
Magnus Pettersson
Mats Pettersson
Mats Wilhelm
Pettersson
Mikael Pettersson
Patrik Pettersson
Tobias Pettersson
Ylva Pettersson
Daniel Piaggio
Strandlund
Ingela Pihlström
Ingrid Plyhm
Linda Pohjola
Kristian Pohl
Toni Poikeljärvi
Joakim Pontén
Maud Ponzio
Karin Porley von Bergen
Karoline Porwoll
Jacob von Post
Jan Erik Posth
Ulrika Pousette
Elena Pravikova
Andy Prhat
Samuel Priedite
Samuel Priedite
Johan Printz
Sami Putkinen
Christer Pålsson
Gun Pålsson
Jörgen Pålsson
Linda Pålsson
Mathias Pålsson
Mats Pärsson
Pekka Pääkkö
Åsa Quesada
Peo Quick
Stewen Quigley
Stefan Qvarnström
María Qwick-Gossas
Sandra Qvist
Hans Qviström
Cecilia Rabnell
Ernest Radal
Martin Ragnar
Jan-Ove Ragnarsson
Staffan Rahm

Makan E-Rahmati
Torbjörn Rambell
Tomas Ramberg
Yvonne Rambring
Håkan Ramsin
Per Ranung
Raúl Raschetti
Björn Rasmussen
Mikael Rasmussen
Ewa Rateitschak Ärlevall
Raila Ratilainen
Katarina Regårdh
Kai Rehn
Anna Rehnberg
Johnny Rehnberg
Ulf Rehnholm
Lennart Rehnman
Vince Reichardt
Göran Reimby
Malin Reinius
Anette Remneby
Christian Renfors
Dennis Renfors
Mikael Reuterswärd
David Reynolds
Ulf Erik Tomas Rhedin
Hana Richtrova
Jana Richtrova
Robert Ridderling
Jonas Ridderström
Daniel Ridings
Srecko Rijetkovic
Anette Rimont
Berndt Rindevall
Hans Ring
Gunnar Risberg
Håkan Risberg
Gisela Ritzén
Malin Robertson Harén
Jan Robertsson
Ronald Robertsson
Olle Robin
Emma Rodling
Claudia Rodriguez
Perdomo
Ulf Rogers
Elke Rogersdotter
Andrzej Roginski
Anna Roginski
Peter Rolén
Erik Rombo
Gudrun Romeborn
Mauro Rongione
Pekka Ronkainen
Yvonne Ronnerfors
Daniel Roos
Gunnar Roos
Joakim Roos
Lars Peter Roos
Eva Roos Sjöqvist
Jan Rosbäck
Lars Rosell
Alf Rosén
Jonas Rosén
Leif Rosén
Mats Rosén

Stina Rosén
Johan Rosenberg
Åsa Rosenberg
Carl Fredrik Rosenblad
Maria Rosengren
Per Rosengren
Ann-Sofi Rosenkvist
Johan Rosenlind
Maria Rosenlöf
Henrik Rosenquist
Marie Rosenqvist
Rune Rosenqvist
Urban Rosenqvist
Anders Rothman
Andreas Rothstein
Jacob M Roupe
Eric Roxfelt
Michelle Roy
Britt Rozental
Mattias Rubin
Malin Rudblom
Carin Rudehill
Håkan Rudels
K-G Rudels
Robin Rundkvist
Martin Runeborg
Hans Åke Runell
Hans Runesson
Kenth Runesson
Carina Ruotsalainen
Paul Russsell
Mikael Rutberg
Peter Rutherhagen
Richard Ryan
Peter Ryberg
Britt-Inger Rydfjäll
Mats Rydsbo
Olov Rydsäter
Anders Ryman
Mårten Ryner
Karin Råghall
Jonas Råsberg
Klara Ränk
Aija Räty
Björn Röhsman
Håkan Röjder
Gustav Rönnbäck
Hans Rönneke
Leif Rönngren
Magdalena Rönström
Anders Rörby
Tobias Röstlund
Can Sahin
Staffan Sahlén
Peter Sahlin
Erkki Saikkonen
Bengt Salander
Claudio Salas
Lina Salomonsson
Petra Salomonsson
Erja-Riitta Salonen
Johan Salwén
Teresa Samuelson
Anna Samuelsson
Fredrik Samuelsson
Hugo Samuelsson

Johnny Samuelsson
Lena Samuelsson
Mats Samuelsson
Olle Sandahl
Barbro Sandberg
Christian Sandberg
David Sandberg
Fredric Sandberg
Hans-Åke Sandberg
Ingvar Sandberg
Magnus Sandberg
Marianne Sandberg
Mats Sandberg
Monica Sandberg
Thorsten Sandberg
Håkan Sandbring
Annalena Sandgren
Maria Sandgren
Sara Sandgren
Mikael Sandholm
David Sandin
Emanuel Sandin
Jakob Sandin
Markus Sandin
Fredrik Sandin Carlson
Katarina Sandqvist
Oskar Sandstedt
Carina Sandström
Johanna Sandström
Mikael Sandström
Stefan Sandström
Susanne Sandström
Micke Sandström
Jens Sandvej Grandin
Paolo Sappei
Garbis H. Sarafian
Anna Sarströmer
Henrik Saxgren
Eric Scarfone
Mats Schagerström
Erik Schale
Marie Schandorph
Forslund
Christoph Schaufelberger
Roger Schederin
Peter Schedwin
Pernilla Schickhardt
Karin Schilt
Kenneth Schlaich
Samuel Schläger
Christoffer Schmiterlöw
Ella Schneider
Richard Schreiner
Eva Schröder
Hasse Schröder
Ursula Schröder
Torsten Schumacher
Marc Schuterman
Lotta Schwarz
Bruno Schwotzer
Jan Schützer
Gunnvor Sebbfolk
Joakim Sebring
Christina Sedelius
Jonas Sedin
Göran Segeholm

Peter Segemark
Lasse Seger
Jennie Segerberg
Mikael Segerby
Erland Segerstedt
Sebastian Sehlén
Bernt Seipl
Daniel Selander
Lisa Selin
Peter Senneryd
Patricia Seoane
Kristiina Sepänmaa
Georg Sessler
Carl Johan von Seth
Mina Sharifiyan
Mohamad Al Sharkawi
Ronnie Sidwall
Ellinore Sigfridsson
Anna Sigge
Sigvard
Anna Sigvardsson
Michal Sikorski
Jan-Åke Siljeström
Maria do Carmo da Silva
  Rocha Petersson
Bo Silwer
Solveig Silverin
Philippe Simon
Anna Simonsson
Martin Simonsson
Mårten Simonsson
Linda Siwerson
Jonas Siöström
Bernt Sjunnesson
David Sjunnesson
Håkan Sjunnesson
Patrik Sjåstad
Christer Sjöberg
Fredrik Sjöberg
Jonas Sjöberg
Josefin Sjöberg
Malin Sjöberg
Maria Sjöberg
Mikael Sjöberg
Olav Sjöberg
Rolf Sjöberg
Sören Sjöberg
Dag Sjöblom
Sigrid Sjöblom
Daniel Sjödahl
Patrik Sjöde
Anders Sjödén
Stellan Sjödén
Olof Sjödin
Anders Sjögren
Sven Sjögren
Anders Sjökvist
Eva Sjökvist
Ingrid Sjökvist
Håkan Sjölund
Johan Sjöquist
Anders Sjöqvist
Sofie Sjöstedt
Svante Sjöstedt
Ulf Sjöstedt
Andreas Sjöström

Håkan Sjöström
Lena Sjöström
Marianne Sjöström
Marie Sjöström
Monica Sjöström
Pernilla Sjöström
Åsa Sjöström
Sanna Sjöswärd
Peter Skallström
Sofia Skanebo
Lars-Göran Skantz
Jostein Skeidsvoll
Urban Skenbäck
Lena Skeppar
Urban Skeppstedt
Kristofer Skog
Andreas Skogh
Per Skoglund
Patrik Skoglöw
Göran Skogsmo
Patrik Skolling Möller
Eric Skoog
Joakim Skoog
Roger Skoog
Anders Skoot
Göran Skyttman
Mårten Skånman
Anders Sköld
Dan Sköld
Roland Sköldblom
Margot Slipare
Angelika Sliwinski
Delia Slotte
Tomas Smedberg
Marianne Smedhäll
Ronnie Smith
Kristian Smålander
Emely Snellman
Per Snellman
Tanya Solorza
Johan Solum
Lisa Sommar-Sandström
Siv Sommelius
Patrik Sonestad
Tedd Soost
Susanna Sorner
Cat Soubbotnik
Titti Spaltro
Maud Spangenberg
Eri-Maria van der Spank
Olle Sporrong
Ola Sprang
Gunilla Staff
Åsa Staffansson
Rolf Staflin
Katarina Stattin
Jimmy Steen
Valentina Stefanoska
Lars Steffenburg
Michael Steinberg
Jonas Stellemark
Göran Stenberg
Henrik Stenberg
Olle Stenberg
Roger Stenberg
Stefan Stenberg

Robert Stenerhag
Johanna Stenius
Susanne Stenius
Erika Stenlund
Staffan Stenlund
Ulrica Stenman
Linnea Stensson
David Stenstad
Gunnel Stenström
Anders Stenudd
Åsa Stenälv
Kjell Sternberg
Fredrik Sterner
Johan Sterner
Maja Sterner
Tobias Sterner
Peter Sterzenbach
David Stiby
Kärsti Stiege
Mikael Stiernstedt
Rose-Marie Stigsdotter
Tinna Stille Öster
Nina Stoetzer
Tommy Stokka
Christer Stolt
Claes Stolt
Hans-Christian Stoltz
Per-Olof Stoltz
Håkan Strand
Mats Strand
Mikael Strand
Per-Olof Strand
Tomas Strand
Ulrika Strand
Gerry Strandberg
Kari Strandberg
Ulf Strandberg
Monica Strandell
Roger Strandell
Annika Strandhed
Håkan Strandman
Ola Strangeways
Roland Stregfeldt
Paul Strehlenert
Bengt-Åke Strengberg
Patrik Strid
Nina Stridh
Heidi Ström
Kurt Ström
Paul Ström
Pär-Magnus Ström
Richard Ström
Martin Ström Savela
Hans Strömberg
Kjell Strömberg
Mia Strömberg
Joakim Strömholm
Håkan Strömquist
Tore Strömquist
Martin Stugholm
Camilla Styrström
Jenny Ståhl
Martin Ståhl
Bosse Ståhlberg
Torsten Ståhlberg
Patrick Ståhle

Christina Stålfors
Mikael Stålsäter
John Stäck
Rickard Sund
Anders Sundberg
Bengt Sundberg
Jonas Sundberg
Magnus Sundberg
Åke Sundelin
Per Gunnar Sundgren
Lars Sundin
Lennart Sundin
Marlene Sundin
Bertil Sundkvist
Kethy Sundlöf Bjesse
Matilda Sundlöv
Stefan Sundman
Karl Erik Sundquist
Leif Sundquist
Elin Sundqvist
Alexander Sundström
Annika Sundvik
Peter Sunesson
Jezzica Sunmo
Krister Surell
Maja Suslin
Saara Suurkuusk
Fredrik Svahn
Göran Svahn
Mårten Svanberg
Sanna Svanberg
Marie Swartz
Gisela Svedberg
Elisabeth Svedin
Kenneth Svedlund
Martina Swedmark
Fredrik Sweger
Bo Svenhammar
Åsa Svennberg
Johan Svenson
Sven-Eric Svenson
Agnes Svensson
Andreas Svensson
Annika Svensson
Ann-Marie Svensson
Bengt-Åke Svensson
Bertil Svensson
Bo Svensson
Camilla Svensson
Carl Axel Svensson
Edith Camilla Svensson
Elisabeth Svensson
Erik G Svensson
Eva Svensson
Eva-Lisa Svensson
Gunilla Svensson
Inger Svensson
Isabelle Svensson
Jacob Svensson
Jelena Svensson
Jonas Svensson
Josefine Svensson
Leif Svensson
Magnus Svensson
Maria Svensson
Mia Svensson

Michael Svensson
Mikael Svensson
Nilsåke Svensson
Petter Svensson
Stefan Svensson
Stig Svensson
Sven-Erik Svensson
Thomas Svensson
Tommy Svensson
Uffe Svensson
Veronika Svensson
Gitta Swetlow-Palecek
Johan Svärd
Manfred Svärd
Mikael Svärdh
Sofi Sykfont
Johanna Syrén
Susanne Sågström
Mats Sålder
Håvard Sæbø
Lars Säfström
Bengt Säll
Jonas Sällberg
Malin Sällberg
Karin Sällström
P-O Sännås
Carl-Johan Söder
Gunilla Söderberg
Gustav Söderberg
Hans Söderberg
Helena Söderberg
Gabriel Söderbladh
Tomas Södergren
Patrik Söderlund
Tommy Söderlund
Birgitta Söderström
Jane Söderström
Laila Söderström
Lena Söderström
Roland Söderström
Stefan Söderström
Axel Sörensen
Christoffer Sörensen
Bo Sörheim
Jenny Sörlin Johansson
Patrick Sörquist
Ivan Taborsak
Karim Taib
Helen Tak
Johanna Tallefors
Ali Tamaddon
Haleh Tamizi
Staffan Tamm
Hanna Tammelin
My Linh Tang
Åse Tangen
Maria Tapper
Jacob Tardell
Eva Tedesjö
Malin Tegelberg
Bosse Teglind
Thomas Teike
Hanna Teleman
Eva Tellander
Didrik Tessier
Anders Thalin

Lisa Thanner
Anna Thanner Olsson
Jacob Thavfelin
Lars Theander
Nicklas Thegerström
Lars Theng
Kristian Thiel
Göran Thisell
Marta Thisner
Johan Thollander
Peter Thomason
Linda Thompson
Ulla Thomsen
Katarina Thorelli
Sonny Thoresen
Johanna Thorsell
Alan Thresh
Elisabeth Throbäck
Lars Thulin
Gunilla Thunberg
Kjell Thunberg
Maria Thunberg
Christina Thuné
Lotta Thunved
Josefine Thuresson
Timea Thurman
Simon Thyr
Susanna Thyselius
Boel Thörn
Carolina Thörn
Charlotta Thörn
Örjan Thöverstam
Robert Tibom
Henrik Tidelius
Iris Tiitto
Karina Tilling
Erik Tinnerwall
Stina Tiselius
Kristina Tjernström
Pernille Tofte
Pia Tofténius
Rick Tomlinson
Erik Torfjäll
Bo-Arne Torger
Ove Torgny
Fredrik Torisson
Ola Torkelsson
Magnus Torle
Jan Torstenson
Patrik Torstensson
Göran Tranåker
Jenny Trobeck
Ingrid Trollsås
Emma Tross
Anders Trossvik
Malin Trotzig
Raymond Tryggvesson
Robert Tryzell
Marie Tsujita
Stephenson
Fredrik Tukk
Anders Tukler
Christoffer Tullgren
Björn Tunberg
Lars Tunbjörk
Susanne Tuomala

Ralf Turander
Roger Turesson
Sigvard Tyge
Björn Tygård
Mats Tylbrant
Sara Tynnerson
Marianne Tyvander
Angelica Tånneryd
Johan Tärbo
Ola Tönnberg
Michael Törnkvist
Christian Törnqvist
Oskar Törnqvist
Christina Uhlin
Valdemar Uhnell
Ensi Ukkola
Dafeamekpor
Maria Ulander
Michael Ulfendahl
Sabina Ulleryd
Björn Ullhagen
Andreas Ulvdell
Björn Unger
Coco Unger
Ingrid Ungerson Kuldvere
Maria Unghanse Tamm
Hillevi Upmanis
Gurli Utas
Maria Uvelöv
Anneli Waara
Gunwi Wadström
Camilla Wagner
Linda Wahl
Filip Wahlberg
Leif Wahlberg
Per Wahlberg
Bo Wahlén
Anna Wahlgren
Magnus Wahlgren
Roine Wahlin
Pernilla Wahlman
Anna Wahlström
Maria Vainionpää
Alex Valcu
Valdemar
Sven Waldemarsson
Andreas Valentin
Eduardo Valenzuela
Tommy Walfridson
Helena Walkhamre
Pernilla Walkhamre
Hans Wall
Karl-Håkan Wall
Katia Wall
Allan Wallberg
Owe Walldin
Petter Wallebo
Jacob Wallenberg
Karolina Wallengren
Lisa Wallenstein
Agneta Wallerman
Jan Wallermark
Örjan Wallers
Mikael Wallerstedt
Conny Wallgren
Anna Wallin

Elin Wallin
Gunnar Wallin
Jimmy Wallin
Johanna Wallin
Mats Wallin
Pierre Wallin
Marcus Wallinder
Magnus Wallman
Christoffer Wallstenius
Gunbritt Wallström
Magnus Wallström
Kim Wallung
Ulrika Walmark
Mia Valtee
Annette Walter
Richard Walter
Anders Walther
Annette Walther
Jonas Valthersson
Björn Wanhatalo
Kaj Wanne
Therése Vare
Lilian Varelamontes
Lina Wargfors
Martin Wargren
Lajos Varhegyi
Klaus Waris
Svante Warping
Curt Warås
Harvey Washbrook
Martin Wasielewski
Patrik Wassberg
Frank Watson
Jan van der veen
Magnus Wegler
Reidun Weigner
Anna-Lena Weintraub
Michael Weintraub
Anders Wejrot
Lars-Olof Welander
Rune Welander
James Velasquez
Xavier Velazquez
Peter Welinder
Sofia Wellborg
Henrik Wellerfors
Heidi Wellstad
Hanna Wemmenhag
Mats Wendelius
Lennart Wennberg
Monica Wennblom
Magnus Wennman
Susanna Wennström
Ylva Werlinder
Ann-Cathrine Wernolf
Lise-Lott Wesslund
Maria Wesström
Emma Westberg
Fredrik Westbom
Elin Wester
Heinz Wester
Ulf Westerberg
Mats Westergren
Ninnie (Ingrid)
Westergren
Anders Westerlund

Berit Westerlund
Lennart Westerlund
Lisbeth Westerlund
Stefan Westerlund
Åsa Westerlund
Ulla Westh
Ellinor Westin
Tommy Westin
Berth Westman
Mikael Westman
Peter Westrup
Hans Wetterfors
Linda Wiberg
Victor Wiberg
Niklas Wibom
Per Wichmann
Fredrik Wicksell
Joakim Victorin
Petro Vidberg
Birgitta Widegren
Thomas Widenberg
Mikael Widerberg
Tintin Vidhammer
Peter Widing
Patric Widlund
Henrik Widman
Bo Widne
Anna Widoff
Sebastian Vidovic
Staffan Widstrand
Tor Wiedling Fernandes
Esko Vierumäki
Lars Wigert
Kjell Wihlborg
Jörgen Wihlner
Svante Wijk
Collette Wijkander
Garrette
Håkan Wikander
Stina Wikberg
Anja Wikén
Pär Wiker
Liv Vikingson
Björn Wiklander
Johan Wiklander
Anders Wiklund
Anna Wiklund
Gustaf Wiklund
Juliana Wiklund
Marie-Louise Wiklund
Peter Wiklund
Sofie Wiklund
Teresa Wiklund
Kenneth Wikman
Niklas Wikman
Lisa Wikstrand
Rune Wikstrand
Charlott Wikström
Elisabeth Wikström
Linda Wikström
Alexander Viktorovich
Håge Wiktorsson
Werner Wildfang
Karin Wildheim
Lars Wildmarker
Marcus Wilhelmsson

Per Wilhelmsson
Stig Vilhelmsson
Per Wilkens
Tom Willhammar
Claes Williamsson
Lisa Wilteus
Samuel Vilör
Ariane Winberg
Thomas Winberg
Sten Winblad
Tina Vincent
Bo-Christer Windenem
Johan Winder
Annika Wink
Sara Winsnes
Jan Eric Wirén
Kristina Wirén
Annah Wirgén
Jan Wiridén
Kai Virihaur
Hans Wising
Katarina Wistrand
Alejandro Vitrera
Henrik Witt
Barbro Vivien
Eva Vogel-Rödin
Camilla Wohlgemuth
Amanuel Workneh
Katarina Wos
Anita Wranell
Fabian Wrede
Ingvar Wretblad
Liz-Marie Wretborn Falk
Dorota Wronkowska
Lasse Vuorio
Cecilia Wågemar
Jesper Wågemar
Tommy Wågemar
Thomas Wågström
Erik Wåhlström
Anders Wånell
Angelica Vägermark
Martin Wänerholm
Ian Vännman
Michael Wärring
Tomas Wässingbo
Margaretha Wästerstam
Sven Wästfelt
Jenny Wästgerd
Anders Wästhed
Jakob Yalgin
Johan Ylitalo
Karin Yllö
Anders Yngström
Rickard Yngwe
Matteus Zablocki
Peter Zachrisson
Zara Zachrisson
Lisbeth Zachs
Linus Zackariasson
Karl-Göran Zahedi
Fougstedt
Dana Zahir
Heinz Zander
Mânica Zander
Magdalena Zeiher Recht

Elisabet Zeilon
Milka Zelic
Thomas Zemturis
Ulf Zetterlund
Mikael Zetterqvist
Grit Zeume
Camilla Zilo
Larsa Zingmark
Pierre Zoetterman
István Zsiga
Ulrica Zwenger
Mikael Zych
Manuel Zyka
Marek Zürn
Eva Åberg
Jan Ågren
Peter Ågren
Carla Åhlander
Anders Åhlund
Eivy Åhlund
Helena Åhlund
Göran Åhs
Linus Åkerlund
Michael Åkerman
Janne Åkesson
Björn Ålander
Martin Åleberg
Klas Åman
Maria Åman
Mikael Ångström
Thomas Årebrand
Åsa Ånfalk-Deleau
Kenneth Åsberg
Yvonne Åsell
Anneli Åsén
Andreas Åsenheim
Christer Åsentorp
Jonnie Åsfjäll
Lennart Åsljung
Christian Åslund
Sebastian Åstrand
Anders Åström
Johan Åström
Lars Åström
Marcus Åström
Sture Åström
Anders Öberg
Daniel Öberg
Hans-Gösta Öberg
Ulla Öberg
Christer Öfverbeck
Anders Öfverström
Annika Öhlund
Dan Öhlund
Frida Öhman
Leif Öhman
Lennart Öhman
Patrik Öhman
Sara Öhman
Magnus Öhnner
Dag Öhrlund
Per Öhström
Susanne Ölund
Ida Ömalm
Svante Örnberg
Johan Örneblad

Per Örnéus
Margaretha Örtengren
Fredrik Örtenholm
Aage Öst
Carin Östberg
Kerstin Östbring
David Öster
Klas Öster
Elias Österberg
Jennie Österberg
Eva Österberg Ericsson
Magnus Österhult
Magnus Österhult
Inga Österman
Viveka Österman
Stefan Östgren
Mattias Östholm
Hans Östlin
Erik Östling
Patrick Östling
Anders R Östlund
Larry Östlund

Postscript

This book is the result of the largest photographic project in Swedish history. The project consists of three parts: the book, an exhibition and last but not least the donation to Sweden's National Archives. Life is largely composed of completely ordinary days, filled with ordinary moments. Yet daily life is documented far too seldom. However, the idea of photographing an entire country in a single day is far from unique. When we founded the Max Ström publishing house almost ten years ago, there were already suggestions that we do something like it here in Sweden. A number of similar books had already been made: A Day in the Life of Australia was published in 1981, and was succeeded by Hawaii (1983), Canada (1984), Japan (1985), USA (1986) and the Soviet Union (1987).

Prompts for Max Ström to produce a Swedish version continued from various quarters. By late 2001, the idea had matured enough for a plan of action. To confirm that there's nothing new under the sun, at our first editorial meeting, our managing editor Lars Fahlén produced a small black and white photo book from 1977 entitled: A Day in the Life of Sweden. Lars had been managing editor at one of Sweden's leading photographic magazines, FOTO, which had asked its readers to document a single day, producing a harvest of more than 2,000 black and white pictures. We were stunned and also proud — long before the other, international projects were conceived, Sweden had its own.

There were several reasons for choosing 3 June as the date for our grand project: we wanted to publish our book in the same year as the pictures were taken so we needed to get the documentation done in the first half of the year. Secondly, we wanted to show Sweden's climate span — in early June, there is still snow in the northern highlands while summer is in full flourish in the south. Thirdly, early June is an intensive period for both working life and leisure while nature is bursting at the seams. And fourthly, taking advice from meteorologist Lage Larsson we discovered that statistically, 3 June is one of the sunniest days of the year. Finally, we wanted the chosen day to be an ordinary weekday, not a weekend or holiday.

It took a full year to prepare; partly in hunting sponsors and partly in organising the small army of photographers. The latter job was huge. We placed advertisements in FOTO magazine and visited photography clubs across the country. We visited most newspapers as well. On top of that, personal letters went out to several hundred photographers and we dumped tons of information flyers at photo labs, camera shops and trade fairs. Response was overwhelming — 3,863 photographers signed up to join the project.

On 3 June, more than one million pictures were snapped for our project. The photographers could submit a maximum of ten pictures; some sent us only one or two, while others sent their full quota. The editorial office was submerged in approximately 24,000 photographs. Photographers competed on equal terms; no one was guaranteed placement in the book or the linked exhibition. True, about forty photographers had been contracted to photograph subject matter that had to be planned in advance, but even their work was subjected to the jury's selection. There were five of us in the jury, invaluably supported by seven picture editors and two assistants, scrutinising every picture. The resulting shortlist was pinned up on large screens along the walls at the studio of Pressens Bild, Sweden's largest picture agency. About a thousand photographs filled the room and from those, the jury made its final choice.

This is a depiction of Sweden and the Swedes by the country's best photographers on the day. In conjunction with publication, an exhibition opened at Kulturhuset — the Cultural Centre — in Stockholm and almost 24,000 pictures were donated to Sweden's National Archives. A gift from Sweden's photographers to future generations.

Marika Stolpe   Jeppe Wikström

A DAY IN THE LIFE OF SWEDEN

Editorial management:
Rolf Adlercreutz, Lars Fahlén, Marika Stolpe,
Jeppe Wikström

Editorial assistant:
Marianne Lindgren

Picture editors:
Rolf Adlercreutz, Stefan Borgius, Lisa Karlsson,
Jens Kristensson, Marianne Lindgren,
Ulrika Pennius, Erik Svensson

Picture assistants:
Helena Gustafsson, Katarina Lindell

Advisory board:
Torbjörn Andersson, Per Lindström,
Britt Marie Mattsson, Hasse Persson

Meteorologist:
Lage Larsson

Art director:
Patric Leo

Layout:
Ylva Magnusson

Jury:
Lars Fahlén, Paul Hansen, Patric Leo,
Marika Stolpe, Jeppe Wikström

Curator:
Ingemar Arnesson, Kulturhuset, Stockholm

Travelling exhibition:
Karin Tengby, Galleri Kontrast, Stockholm

Colour separation:
Anders Fasth, John Nelander, Johan Eklund

Printing management:
Magnus Almgren, Tomas Ek

For professional use of pictures from the book,
please contact Pressens Bild in Stockholm